Quantitative Finance
Interview Questions and Answers

X.Y. Wang

Contents

Chapter 1

Introduction

Welcome to "Quantitative Finance Interview Questions and Answers," the ultimate guide to help you excel in interviews and deepen your understanding of the ever-evolving world of quantitative finance. This book is designed to be an invaluable resource for students, job-seekers, and professionals alike who are interested in pursuing a career in the quantitative finance industry.

The field of quantitative finance has grown exponentially in recent years due to the rapid advancements in computing power, big data, and machine learning. As a result, financial institutions increasingly rely on quantitative models to analyze financial data, manage risk, and develop investment strategies. As such, possessing a solid understanding of quantitative finance concepts and techniques has become essential for those who aspire to thrive in this dynamic and competitive industry.

This book is structured into five progressive sections – Basic, Intermediate, Advanced, Expert, and Guru – to suit readers with varying levels of expertise. Each section contains a comprehensive collection of questions and answers that cover a wide range of topics, including financial asset types, risk management, portfolio optimization, derivative pricing, machine learning, and high-frequency trading, among many others.

The questions and answers in this book have been meticulously curated and crafted by experts in the field to ensure that the content is up-to-date, relevant, and accurate. This book aims to provide a solid foundation for readers to build upon, enabling them to tackle even the most challenging quantitative finance problems with confidence.

Whether you are a student seeking to enhance your understanding of quantitative finance, a professional preparing for a job interview, or an expert looking to brush up on your knowledge, this book is an indispensable resource. As you delve into the chapters, you will acquire a deeper understanding of the core concepts and techniques that underpin quantitative finance, empowering you to excel in interviews and advance your career in this exciting and rewarding field.

So, let's begin your journey to mastering quantitative finance with "Quantitative Finance Interview Questions and Answers."

Chapter 2

Basic

2.1   What is quantitative finance and how does it differ from traditional finance?

Quantitative finance is an interdisciplinary field that combines financial theory, mathematical models, statistical analysis, and computer programming to solve complex financial problems. It emerged in the 1970s in response to the increasing complexity and sophistication of financial markets, instruments and institutions. A key objective of quantitative finance is to create mathematical models that can be used to represent financial instruments and price them accurately. The field has come to encompass a wide range of topics, including options pricing, risk management, portfolio optimization, trading strategies and financial engineering.

Quantitative finance differs from traditional finance in its use of advanced mathematical models and computer simulations to analyze financial problems. In traditional finance, decisions are often made based on intuition and judgment, whereas in quantitative finance, decisions are based on rigorous analysis and optimization using mathematical and computational tools. Quantitative finance also places much greater emphasis on risk management, using statistical models and simulations to understand the potential downside of different investment strategies.

As an example, consider the task of pricing an option, which is a financial contract that gives the holder the right (but not the obligation) to buy or sell an underlying asset at a specified price and date. In traditional finance, the pricing of options is often based on theoretical models such as Black-Scholes, which make simplifying assumptions about the behavior of financial markets. In quantitative finance, however, pricing models are built using more advanced mathematics, such as stochastic calculus and partial differential equations. These models allow for a more realistic representation of market behavior, leading to more accurate pricing of options.

Overall, quantitative finance allows for a more rigorous and systematic approach to financial analysis, which can help investors and financial institutions make better decisions and manage risks more effectively.

2.2   What are the main types of financial assets?

Financial assets are any assets that represent an ownership interest in an entity or a contractual right to receive or provide cash. There are several main types of financial assets:

1. Stocks (Equities): Stocks represent ownership in a company. When you buy a stock, you become a shareholder and own a portion of the company. The value of a stock is determined by the company's financial performance and the supply and demand for the stock in the market. Stocks can generate returns through capital appreciation and dividends.

2. Bonds (Fixed Income): A bond is a debt instrument issued by a company or government entity. When you buy a bond, you are essentially lending money to the issuer. Bonds typically pay interest periodically and return the principal amount at maturity. Bond prices are affected by changes in interest rates and credit risk.

3. Cash and Cash Equivalents: Cash and cash equivalents are highly liquid assets that can be easily converted into cash. Examples include savings accounts, money market funds, and short-term government bonds.

4. Derivatives: A derivative is a financial instrument whose value is derived from the value of an underlying asset. Common examples of derivatives include options, futures contracts, and swaps. Derivatives are used for hedging, speculation, and investment purposes.

5. Real Estate: Real estate represents an ownership interest in a physical property such as a house, apartment, or commercial building. Real estate can generate returns through rental income and capital appreciation.

There are also other types of financial assets such as commodities, mutual funds, exchange-traded funds (ETFs), and alternative investments. Investors typically hold a portfolio of different types of financial assets to diversify their risk and achieve their investment goals.

2.3   What is the time value of money, and why is it important?

The time value of money is the concept that money available at the present time is worth more than the same amount of money in the future. This is due to the fact that money available in the present can be invested and earn interest, while money in the future cannot. Therefore, if given the choice between receiving $100 now or receiving $100 a year from now, most people would choose to receive the money now because the value of money decreases over time due to inflation and opportunity cost.

This concept is extremely important in finance, as it allows individuals and businesses to make informed decisions regarding investments, loans, and other financial opportunities. By understanding the time value of money, investors can assess the potential return on investment of different opportunities and make decisions based on their individual risk preferences.

In order to calculate the time value of money, several factors must be taken into account, including the interest rate, the length of time the money will be invested or borrowed, and the expected rate of inflation. These factors are then used to calculate the present value or future value of an investment or loan.

For example, suppose an investor has an opportunity to invest $1,000 for five years at an annual interest rate of 5%. Using the formula for calculating the future value of an investment, we can determine that the future value of the investment will be:

$$FV = PV * (1 + r)^n$$

Where FV is the future value, PV is the present value, r is the interest rate and n is the number of periods.

$$FV = 1,000 * (1 + .05)^5 = \$1,276.28$$

This means that in five years, the investor's initial investment of $1,000 will have grown to $1,276.28 due to the effects of interest.

On the other hand, if an individual takes out a loan for $1,000 at an annual interest rate of 5% to be paid back in five years, the present value of the loan can be calculated using the formula for present value:

$$PV = FV/(1 + r)^n$$

Where PV is the present value, FV is the future value, r is the interest rate, and n is the number of periods.

$$PV = 1,000/(1 + .05)^5 = \$784.00$$

This means that the individual would need to pay back $1,000 plus an additional $216 in interest over the course of five years.

Overall, understanding the time value of money is crucial in making informed financial decisions and can have a significant impact on an individual's or business's financial well-being.

2.4   What is the difference between simple and compound interest? Can you provide an example?

Simple interest is the type of interest that is calculated on the principal amount only, while compound interest is calculated on the principal amount plus any interest earned over time.

The formula for simple interest can be represented as follows:

$$I = P \cdot r \cdot t$$

where:

- I is the interest
- P is the principal amount
- r is the rate of interest
- t is the time period

For example, if you invest $1,000 at a simple annual interest rate of 5% for three years, the interest earned would be calculated as follows:

$$I = 1000 \cdot 0.05 \cdot 3 = 150$$

Therefore, the total amount to be paid after three years would be $1,150.

On the other hand, the formula for compound interest can be represented as follows:

$$A = P \cdot \left(1 + \frac{r}{n}\right)^{nt}$$

where:

- A is the total amount after n years
- P is the principal amount
- r is the annual interest rate
- n is the number of times interest is compounded per year
- t is the number of years

For example, if you invest \$1,000 at a rate of 5% compounded annually for three years, the total amount earned would be calculated as follows:

$$A = 1000 \cdot \left(1 + \frac{0.05}{1}\right)^{1 \cdot 3} = 1157.63$$

Therefore, the total amount to be paid after three years would be \$1,157.63.

As you can see from the above example, compound interest generates more returns than simple interest for the same principal amount, interest rate, and time period. That is why most loan and investment products use compound interest.

2.5   What is the concept of present value and future value in finance?

The concept of present value and future value are fundamental to finance and have a significant impact on various financial applications.

Present Value (PV) refers to the current value of a future cash flow or a stream of cash flows that are expected to be received over time. In other words, it is the amount of money that would be required today to produce the same cash flows in the future. The present value is affected by various factors such as the interest rate, the number of periods, and the size of the cash flow.

Mathematically, the present value of a future cash flow can be calculated using the following formula:

$$PV = \frac{FV}{(1+r)^n}$$

where PV is the present value, FV is the future value, r is the interest rate and n is the number of periods.

For example, let's assume that an individual plans to receive $1,000 in two years, and the annual interest rate is 5%. The present value of this future cash flow can be calculated as follows:

$$PV = \frac{1,000}{(1+0.05)^2} = \$907.03$$

This means that if the individual wants to have $1,000 in two years, they would need to invest $907.03 today at a 5% interest rate.

On the other hand, Future Value (FV) refers to the value of an investment at a specified date in the future. It represents the amount that an investment will grow to over time, assuming a fixed interest rate. Future value can be calculated by applying compound interest to an investment or a stream of cash flows over time.

Mathematically, the future value of an investment can be calculated using the following formula:

$$FV = PV * (1 + r)^n$$

where FV is the future value, PV is the present value, r is the interest rate and n is the number of periods.

For example, if an individual invests $1,000 today at an annual interest rate of 5% for two years, the future value of the investment can be calculated as follows:

$$FV = \$1,000 * (1 + 0.05)^2 = \$1,102.50$$

This means that the investment would grow to $1,102.50 in two years, assuming a fixed interest rate of 5%.

In conclusion, understanding the concepts of present value and future value is essential in finance as it helps individuals and businesses make informed investment decisions, assess the value of assets and liabilities, and calculate future cash flows.

2.6   Can you explain the difference between risk and uncertainty in finance?

In finance, the terms "risk" and "uncertainty" are often used interchangeably, but they have different meanings.

Risk refers to the probability or likelihood of an event occurring and the impact it would have if it did occur. It is something that can be quantified and measured using statistical tools. For example, the risk of a stock price falling by 10% in a day can be calculated based on historical data and the current market conditions.

Uncertainty, on the other hand, refers to situations where the probability or likelihood of an event cannot be quantified, either because of lack of information or because the event has never occurred before. Uncertainty is common in financial markets, where unexpected events such as geopolitical tensions, natural disasters, or unexpected changes in policy can impact prices in unpredictable ways.

While risk can be managed, uncertainty is more difficult to manage because of its unpredictable nature. However, diversification and risk management strategies can help investors build resilience and reduce the impact of uncertain events on their portfolios.

To illustrate the difference between risk and uncertainty, consider the example of investing in a stock. The risk of investing in a stock can be calculated based on past performance and current market conditions, such as the company's financial health, the outlook for its industry, and broader economic trends. Uncertainty, on the other hand, can arise from unexpected events such as a new competitor entering the market, a change in government policy, or a natural disaster that disrupts the company's supply chain. While risk can be managed through diversification and other strategies, uncertainty requires more flexible and adaptive approaches to investment management.

2.7   What is diversification, and why is it important in portfolio management?

Diversification is a risk management strategy that involves spreading investments across multiple assets, such as stocks, bonds, and commodities, in order to reduce the overall risk of a portfolio. The basic premise behind diversification is that different asset classes have different return and risk characteristics, and by combining these assets in a portfolio, an investor can achieve a more balanced risk-return profile.

The importance of diversification in portfolio management stems from the fact that every investment carries inherent risk. If an investor puts all of their money into a single stock, for example, they are essentially betting their entire portfolio on the performance of that one company. If the company performs poorly or suffers significant losses, the investor's entire portfolio could be wiped out. On the other hand, if the investor spreads their investments across multiple stocks, as well as other asset classes, they can reduce the impact of any one investment on their overall portfolio.

Diversification can also help to maximize returns over the long term. Although diversification cannot eliminate risk entirely, it can help to minimize the impact of market fluctuations, and reduce the overall volatility of a portfolio. By doing so, investors may be able to achieve more stable returns over time, even in the face of market downturns.

One way to achieve diversification is through asset allocation, in which an investor divides their portfolio into different asset classes, such as stocks, bonds, and cash, and then allocates a certain percentage of their funds to each category. Another common diversification strategy is to invest in a variety of different companies within a particular asset class, such as stocks in different sectors, or bonds with varying credit ratings.

Overall, diversification is a critical aspect of portfolio management, and one that can help investors to achieve a more balanced and stable risk-return profile over the long term.

2.8   What is the efficient market hypothesis (EMH)?

The efficient market hypothesis (EMH) is a theory that suggests that financial markets quickly and efficiently incorporate all available information into asset prices. Therefore, it is impossible to consistently achieve returns above the average market return, unless it is due to chance or the acceptance of greater risk. The EMH is a cornerstone of modern financial economics and has implications for investment strategy, risk management, and financial regulation.

There are three forms of the EMH: weak, semi-strong, and strong.

The weak form of the EMH posits that current market prices

fully reflect all historical prices and any publicly available trading information, such as trading volume and bid-ask spreads. Therefore, technical analysis or the study of historical prices cannot be used to consistently generate excess returns.

The semi-strong form of the EMH suggests that stock prices quickly and efficiently incorporate all public information, including company announcements, financial statements, and economic data. Therefore, fundamental analysis or the study of financial and economic data cannot be consistently used to generate excess returns.

The strong form of the EMH is the most demanding version and suggests that all information, both public and private, is already reflected in market prices. Therefore, insider trading or the use of non-public information cannot be used to generate excess returns.

The EMH has important implications for investors and financial professionals as it suggests that it is difficult or impossible to consistently generate above-market returns through either technical or fundamental analysis. However, some critics have argued that the EMH is not entirely accurate, as there are instances where inefficiencies and anomalies exist in financial markets, which can be exploited through various trading strategies. These anomalies include the momentum effect, value effect, and the low-volatility anomaly. Overall, the EMH remains a controversial topic in finance that has significant implications for investment strategy and financial decision-making.

2.9   Can you provide a brief overview of modern portfolio theory (MPT)?

Modern Portfolio Theory (MPT) is a framework used for constructing investment portfolios by optimizing the trade-off between expected returns and risk faced by an investor. It is based on the premise that the expected return of a portfolio should not only consider the returns of individual assets but also take into account the correlation between those returns.

The fundamental principle of MPT is diversification- the idea that an investor can reduce risk by holding a portfolio of investments that are not perfectly correlated. The goal of MPT is to find the optimal portfolio, which is the portfolio that offers the highest expected return for a given level of risk, or the lowest level of risk for a given expected return.

MPT involves several steps, including:

1. Asset allocation: This is the process of deciding how to allocate investment capital across different asset classes such as stocks, bonds, commodities, real estate, etc. The allocation is based on the investor's risk tolerance, investment horizon, and expected returns for each asset class.

2. Risk assessment: This is the process of assessing the risk of individual assets and the portfolio as a whole. Risk is typically measured by the standard deviation of returns, which is a measure of the volatility of an asset's returns over time.

3. Portfolio optimization: This is the process of constructing a portfolio that maximizes expected returns for a given level of risk or minimizes risk for a given level of expected returns. The

optimal portfolio is usually found by solving the mean-variance optimization problem, which involves finding the portfolio with the highest expected return for a given level of risk, or the lowest level of risk for a given expected return.

4. Performance monitoring: Once the portfolio is constructed, it's crucial to monitor its performance regularly and make adjustments if necessary to keep it aligned with the investor's goals.

In summary, MPT provides a framework for building investment portfolios that optimize the trade-off between expected returns and risk. It's based on the principle of diversification, which reduces risk by holding investments that are not perfectly correlated.

2.10 What are the main types of financial derivatives, and how are they used?

Financial derivatives are financial instruments whose value is derived from the value of an underlying asset, such as stocks, bonds, commodities, currencies, or indices. They provide market participants with a way to manage risk, speculate on price movements, and gain exposure to various markets or assets without owning them directly.

There are many types of financial derivatives, but some of the main ones include:

1. Futures contracts: Futures contracts are standardized agreements to buy or sell an underlying asset at a specified price and date in the future. Futures contracts are traded on organized

exchanges and are used by market participants to hedge against price fluctuations or to speculate on price movements. For example, a farmer might sell futures contracts for their crop to guarantee a minimum price, while a speculator might buy futures contracts to profit from an anticipated price increase.

2. Options: Options contracts give the holder the right, but not the obligation, to buy (call option) or sell (put option) an underlying asset at a specified price and date in the future. Options contracts can be used to hedge against price movements or to speculate on market outcomes. For example, an investor might buy call options on a stock they expect will rise in price, or buy put options on a stock they expect will decrease in price.

3. Swaps: Swaps are agreements between two parties to exchange cash flows based on the performance of an underlying asset. The most common type of swap is an interest rate swap, where two parties agree to exchange fixed and floating interest rate payments based on a notional principal amount. Swaps can be used to manage interest rate risk, currency risk, and credit risk.

4. Credit derivatives: Credit derivatives are financial instruments that allow investors to hedge against credit risk or to speculate on default events. The most common type of credit derivative is a credit default swap (CDS), which is an agreement between two parties where one party agrees to pay the other party in the event of a credit event, such as a default or bankruptcy.

5. Equity derivatives: Equity derivatives are financial instruments that are based on the performance of stocks or stock indices. The most common type of equity derivative is a stock option, which gives the holder the right to buy or sell a stock

at a specified price and date in the future. Equity derivatives can be used to hedge against stock market risk, to speculate on price movements, or to gain exposure to specific markets or sectors.

Overall, financial derivatives play a crucial role in modern financial markets by providing market participants with a way to manage risk and gain exposure to various markets or assets. However, they also carry risks of their own, such as counterparty risk, liquidity risk, and operational risk, and require careful management and oversight.

2.11   What is the Black-Scholes model, and what does it help to calculate?

The Black-Scholes model is a mathematical model used to calculate the theoretical value of European-style call and put options. It was developed by Fischer Black and Myron Scholes in 1973 and later extended by Robert Merton. The model assumes that the underlying asset follows a geometric Brownian motion and that the risk-free rate, volatility, and time to expiration are all known and constant.

The model helps to calculate the fair value of options by taking into account five input variables:

1. Underlying asset price: This is the current market price of the underlying asset, such as a stock or a commodity.

2. Strike price: This is the predetermined price at which the option holder has the right to buy or sell the underlying asset.

3. Time to expiration: This is the time remaining until the option expires, and the holder must exercise their right to buy or sell the underlying asset.

4. Risk-free rate: This is the rate of return on a risk-free investment, such as U.S. Treasury bonds, that the option holder can earn over the life of the option.

5. Volatility: This is a measure of how much the underlying asset's price fluctuates over time. Options on assets that are more volatile are generally more expensive.

Using these input variables, the Black-Scholes model calculates the theoretical price of a call or put option. The formula for calculating the fair value of a European call option using the Black-Scholes model is:

$$C = S_0 N(d_1) - Ke^{-rT} N(d_2)$$

where:

- C is the fair value of the call option
- S0 is the current market price of the underlying asset
- K is the strike price
- r is the risk-free rate
- T is the time to expiration
- N() is the cumulative standard normal distribution function
- d1 and d2 are calculated as follows:

$$d_1 = \frac{\ln\left(\frac{S_0}{K}\right) + \left(r + \frac{\sigma^2}{2}\right)T}{\sigma\sqrt{T}}$$

$$d_2 = d_1 - \sigma\sqrt{T}$$

The formula for calculating the fair value of a put option is similar but involves different inputs:

$$P = Ke^{-rT}N(-d_2) - S_0N(-d_1)$$

where P is the fair value of the put option.

In summary, the Black-Scholes model provides a mathematical framework for determining the fair value of options based on various input variables. It is widely used by option traders and investors to estimate the value of options and to make informed trading decisions.

2.12 What are the main types of financial risk, and how can they be managed?

There are several types of financial risks that businesses and investors face:

1. Market Risk: Market risk is the most common type of financial risk, and it refers to the risk of financial loss resulting from changes in the value of financial instruments such as stocks,

bonds, and currencies. This risk can be managed through diversification, hedging, and risk management strategies such as stop-loss orders.

2. Credit Risk: Credit risk refers to the risk of loss resulting from the failure of a debtor to honor their financial obligations. This risk can be managed through credit analysis, diversification of the portfolio, and the use of credit derivatives such as credit default swaps.

3. Liquidity Risk: Liquidity risk refers to the risk of loss resulting from the inability to execute a trade quickly enough or at a favorable price. This risk can be managed through maintaining sufficient cash reserves, establishing credit lines, and using market-making strategies.

4. Operational Risk: Operational risk refers to the risk of loss resulting from internal or external events such as system failures, fraud, or catastrophic events such as natural disasters. This risk can be managed through effective internal controls, contingency planning, and insurance.

5. Reputational Risk: Reputational risk refers to the risk of loss resulting from damage to a company's reputation. This risk can be managed through effective communication, monitoring of public perception, and the implementation of proactive risk management strategies.

In addition to these types of risks, there are also other types of risks such as political, legal, and regulatory risks. These risks can be managed through political analysis, legal compliance, and other risk management strategies.

Overall, risk management is an important process that involves identifying and measuring risks, developing risk management strategies, and continuously monitoring and adjusting these strategies to minimize the impact of financial risk. By effectively managing financial risk, businesses and investors can reduce the potential for financial loss and maximize their returns.

2.13 What is the difference between systematic and unsystematic risk?

In finance, risk can generally be classified into two types, systematic risk and unsystematic risk.

Systematic risk refers to the risk that affects the overall market or a specific market segment, and is therefore unavoidable. It is also known as market risk, economy-wide risk, or non-diversifiable risk. This kind of risk cannot be reduced through diversification because it is inherent in the overall market. Systematic risk factors include changes in interest rates, economic growth, and geopolitical events.

Unsystematic risk, on the other hand, refers to the risk that affects a specific company or industry, and can be reduced or eliminated through diversification. It is also known as specific risk or diversifiable risk. Unsystematic risk factors include company-specific events such as a management change, a product recall, or a lawsuit against the company.

For example, if an investor invests in a single stock, they face unsystematic risk because the stock's return could be affected by factors specific to that company, such as poor management decisions or a decline in demand for its products. However, if the investor also invests in a diversified portfolio of stocks, then the unsystematic risk is reduced because the negative impact of any one company-specific event is spread out across the portfolio.

The distinction between systematic and unsystematic risk is important for investors when making investment decisions. Investors aim to minimize risk through diversification, and by understanding the sources of risk, they can make more informed decisions about the allocation of their investments.

2.14   What are the main types of financial ratios, and how are they used in financial analysis?

Financial ratios are measures used to evaluate and compare the financial performance of a company. They are widely used by investors, creditors, and analysts to assess a company's financial health, profitability, liquidity, solvency, and operating efficiency. There are different types of financial ratios that are used to evaluate different aspects of a company's performance. In this answer, I will discuss the main types of financial ratios and how they are used in financial analysis.

1. Liquidity ratios
Liquidity ratios are used to measure a company's ability to meet its short-term obligations. These ratios indicate whether a company has sufficient short-term assets to cover its short-term liabilities. The two main liquidity ratios are the current ratio and the quick ratio.

- Current ratio = Current assets / Current liabilities

The current ratio measures a company's ability to meet its short-term obligations using its current assets. A ratio of 1 or higher is considered good, indicating that the company has enough current assets to cover its current liabilities.

- Quick ratio = (Current assets - Inventory) / Current liabilities
The quick ratio measures a company's ability to meet its short-term obligations using its most liquid assets (excluding inventory). A quick ratio of 1 or higher is considered good, indicating that the company has enough liquid assets to cover its short-term liabilities.

2. Solvency ratios
Solvency ratios are used to measure a company's ability to meet its long-term obligations. These ratios indicate whether a company has sufficient long-term assets to cover its long-term liabilities. The two main solvency ratios are the debt-to-equity ratio and the interest coverage ratio.

- Debt-to-equity ratio = Total debt / Total equity
The debt-to-equity ratio measures a company's leverage or its degree of indebtedness. A high ratio indicates that the company has more debt than equity, which may make it more risky.

- Interest coverage ratio = Earnings before interest and taxes (EBIT) / Interest expense
The interest coverage ratio measures a company's ability to service its interest payments from its earnings. A ratio of 1.5 or higher is considered good, indicating that the company has enough earnings to cover its interest expenses.

3. Profitability ratios
Profitability ratios are used to measure a company's ability to generate profits. These ratios indicate how efficiently a com-

pany is utilizing its resources to generate profits. The three main profitability ratios are the gross profit margin, the operating profit margin, and the net profit margin.

- Gross profit margin = Gross profit / Revenue
The gross profit margin measures the percentage of revenue that is left after deducting the cost of goods sold. A higher gross profit margin indicates that the company is generating more profit from its sales.

- Operating profit margin = Operating profit / Revenue
The operating profit margin measures the percentage of revenue that is left after deducting all operating expenses. A higher operating profit margin indicates that the company is generating more profit from its operations.

- Net profit margin = Net profit / Revenue
The net profit margin measures the percentage of revenue that is left after deducting all expenses, including taxes and interest. A higher net profit margin indicates that the company is generating more profit from its overall operations.

4. Efficiency ratios
Efficiency ratios are used to measure a company's ability to utilize its assets and resources efficiently. These ratios indicate how well a company is managing its assets to generate revenue. The two main efficiency ratios are the asset turnover ratio and the inventory turnover ratio.

- Asset turnover ratio = Revenue / Total assets
The asset turnover ratio measures the amount of revenue generated for every dollar invested in assets. A higher asset turnover ratio indicates that the company is efficiently utilizing its assets to generate revenue.

- Inventory turnover ratio = Cost of goods sold / Average inventory

The inventory turnover ratio measures how many times a company's inventory is sold and replaced during a period. A higher inventory turnover ratio indicates that the company is efficiently managing its inventory.

In conclusion, financial ratios are important tools for financial analysis, providing insights into a company's financial health and performance. Different types of ratios are used to evaluate different aspects of a company's performance, including liquidity, solvency, profitability, and efficiency. By comparing a company's ratios to industry averages and historical trends, investors and analysts can assess its financial position and make informed investment decisions.

2.15 What is the Capital Asset Pricing Model (CAPM), and how is it used in finance?

The Capital Asset Pricing Model (CAPM) is a widely-used financial model that attempts to explain the relationship between risk and expected return for individual securities or portfolios.

The basic intuition behind the CAPM is that investors demand a higher return for taking on higher levels of risk. In other words, if investors can invest in a security with lower risk and achieve the same return as a security with higher risk, they would prefer the lower-risk security. The CAPM provides a way to quantify how much extra return investors should expect to receive for taking on additional risk.

The CAPM formula can be expressed as:

$$E(R_i) = R_f + \beta_i(E(R_m) - R_f)$$

where:

- $E(R_i)$ is the expected return for security i
- R_f is the risk-free rate of return
- β_i is the systematic (market) risk of security i
- $E(R_m)$ is the expected return of the market portfolio

The basic idea is that the expected return for a security is equal to the risk-free rate plus a risk premium, where the risk premium is proportional to the systematic (market) risk of the security, as measured by its beta.

In practice, the CAPM is often used to estimate the expected return of a security or portfolio, given its estimated beta and the market risk premium (i.e. the difference between the expected return of the market portfolio and the risk-free rate). This expected return can then be used as a benchmark for evaluating whether the security or portfolio is overvalued or undervalued, based on its current market price.

The CAPM has some limitations, including the assumption of a single factor (the market) driving security returns, and the assumptions of rational and homogeneous investors. However, it remains a widely-used tool in finance for evaluating risk and return, particularly in the context of portfolio management and asset pricing.

2.16   What is the difference between technical and fundamental analysis?

Technical analysis and fundamental analysis are both widely used methods for analyzing financial markets. Technical analysts believe that the price of an asset reflects all available information, whereas fundamental analysts believe that the price of an asset may not reflect its true value and that it is necessary to analyze the underlying economic and financial factors that affect its value.

Technical analysis is the study of past market data, primarily price and volume, in order to identify patterns and trends that can be used to predict future price movements. Technical analysts use charts and technical indicators to analyze this data, with the aim of determining the direction of future price movements. Technical analysis is often used in short-term trading, where the focus is on identifying short-term price movements that can be exploited for profit.

Fundamental analysis, on the other hand, is the study of the economic, financial and other qualitative and quantitative factors that affect the value of an asset. This can include factors such as a company's financial performance, industry trends, macroeconomic indicators, and other factors that can have an impact on the underlying value of an asset. Fundamental analysis is often used in longer-term investing, where the focus is on identifying undervalued or overvalued assets based on their underlying fundamentals.

To illustrate the difference between technical and fundamental analysis, consider the example of a stock. A technical analyst might look at the stock's past price movements and volume data to try to identify patterns that suggest a trend in the stock's price direction. They might use technical indicators such as moving averages, Relative Strength Index (RSI) and Bollinger Bands to help identify potential buy or sell signals. A fundamental analyst, on the other hand, would focus on the underlying financial performance of the company, looking at factors such as earnings growth, revenue growth, debt levels, and other financial metrics to determine whether the stock is undervalued or overvalued compared to its peers.

In summary, technical analysis is based on the study of past price and volume data, while fundamental analysis is based on the analysis of the underlying economic and financial factors that affect an asset's value. Both methods have their strengths and weaknesses, and many traders and investors use a combination of both approaches to make informed decisions.

2.17   Can you explain what a bond is and how its price is determined?

A bond is a type of fixed-income security that represents a loan made by an investor to a borrower (typically a corporation or government). The bond issuer agrees to pay the bondholder a fixed interest rate, known as the coupon rate, on a predetermined schedule for a specified period of time, called the bond's maturity. At maturity, the issuer returns the face value of the bond to the bondholder.

The price of a bond is primarily determined by supply and demand in the market. When the bond is first issued, it has an initial price or face value, typically $1,000, which is also known as the par value or principal value. This initial price is determined by the issuer based on prevailing interest rates, creditworthiness of the issuer, and other market factors.

Subsequently, the price of a bond can fluctuate in response to changes in interest rates, credit ratings, economic conditions, or investor demand. When interest rates rise, the price of existing bonds falls because the coupon rate on those bonds is now relatively less attractive compared to newly issued bonds with higher coupon rates. Conversely, when interest rates fall, the price of existing bonds rises, making them more attractive to investors.

To illustrate this relationship, consider the case of a $1,000 bond with a coupon rate of 5% and a maturity of 10 years. If prevailing interest rates rise to 6%, a new bond with a coupon rate of 6% would be more attractive to investors, as it would offer a higher yield. Consequently, the price of the 5% bond would fall below par to compensate for the relative unattractiveness of its coupon rate. The extent of the price drop would depend on the bond's duration or sensitivity to changes in interest rates.

Bond prices can also be affected by changes in the issuer's credit rating or perceived risk. When an issuer's financial health deteriorates or other economic conditions change, the market may view the issuer as more risky, causing investors to demand a higher return (i.e., a higher coupon rate) to compensate for the increased risk. This can cause the price of the bond to decline, as its coupon rate becomes relatively less attractive.

In general, the price of a bond can be thought of as the present value of its future cash flows, including both coupon payments and the face value at maturity. To calculate the present value, investors discount the future cash flows by an appropriate interest rate determined by prevailing market conditions. This is known as the bond's yield to maturity, which is the internal rate of return that makes the present value of the bond's cash flows equal to its current market price.

Overall, the price of a bond is influenced by various factors, including prevailing interest rates, credit ratings, economic conditions, and investor demand. It is important for investors to carefully evaluate these factors when making investment decisions in the bond market.

2.18   What are the main types of option contracts, and what are their key features?

There are two main types of option contracts: call options and put options. Both types of options give the holder the right, but not the obligation, to buy (in the case of a call option) or sell (in the case of a put option) an underlying asset at a predetermined price (called the strike price) on or before a specified date (called the expiration date).

Call Options
Call options are contracts that give buyers the right, but not the obligation, to buy the underlying asset at the strike price on or before the expiration date. Call options are typically used to profit from an expected increase in the price of the underlying asset or as a hedge against a short position in the underlying asset.

The buyer of a call option pays a premium to the seller of

the option. The seller of a call option is obligated to sell the underlying asset to the buyer if the buyer chooses to exercise the option. The seller of the option receives the premium paid by the buyer, regardless of whether the option is exercised or not.

For example, suppose you buy a call option on a stock with a strike price of $50 and an expiration date of 3 months from now for a premium of $2. If the stock price rises to $60 before the expiration date, you can exercise your call option and buy the stock for $50, then immediately sell the stock on the open market for $60, making a profit of $8 per share.

Put Options
Put options are contracts that give buyers the right, but not the obligation, to sell the underlying asset at the strike price on or before the expiration date. Put options are typically used to profit from an expected decrease in the price of the underlying asset or as a hedge against a long position in the underlying asset.

The buyer of a put option pays a premium to the seller of the option. The seller of a put option is obligated to buy the underlying asset from the buyer if the buyer chooses to exercise the option. The seller of the option receives the premium paid by the buyer, regardless of whether the option is exercised or not.

For example, suppose you buy a put option on a stock with a strike price of $50 and an expiration date of 3 months from now for a premium of $2. If the stock price falls to $40 before the expiration date, you can exercise your put option and sell the stock for $50, then immediately buy the stock back on the open market for $40, making a profit of $8 per share.

In summary, call options give the holder the right to buy an underlying asset while put options give the holder the right to sell an underlying asset. Both types of options have their own unique risks and rewards, and are often used by investors to manage risk or to take advantage of market opportunities.

2.19   What is the role of a central bank in the financial system?

A central bank is a critical player in any financial system, and its role usually includes some, if not all, of the following:

1. Implementing Monetary Policy: A central bank's primary role is to manage a country's monetary policy. To do so, a central bank typically sets interest rates or adjusts the money supply to control inflation, stabilize the economy, and promote growth. When there is inflation, the central bank may increase interest rates to reduce the money supply, which would lower demand and bring prices back down. Conversely, when there is a recession, the central bank may lower interest rates to stimulate the economy, increase borrowing, and inject cash into the economy to spur growth.

2. Regulating and Supervising Financial Institutions: The central bank may also supervise and regulate financial institutions within the country. The central bank's supervisory function is crucial to ensure that these institutions operate in a stable and solvent manner and comply with established policies and regulations.

3. Providing Financial Services: Central banks provide essential financial services, such as managing the nation's currency,

providing loans to other banks or the government, and managing foreign exchange reserves.

4. Ensuring Financial Stability: Central banks play a critical role in ensuring financial stability. They monitor the health of the financial system, identify potential risks, and take action to prevent and mitigate systemic risks that could threaten the stability of the financial system.

5. Supporting the Economic Development: Central banks may also play a critical role in supporting economic development, such as financing infrastructure projects and providing support to SMEs.

For example, let's consider the case of the United States Federal Reserve (Fed). One of the Fed's primary roles is to implement monetary policy by setting interest rates and influencing the money supply. During the 2008 financial crisis, the Fed lowered interest rates to near-zero to stimulate the economy and save financial institutions that were on the verge of collapse.

In addition to its monetary policy role, the Fed also regulates and supervises financial institutions to ensure that they operate in a safe and sound manner. The Fed also provides essential financial services, such as managing the nation's currency and providing loans to other banks.

Overall, a central bank's role is critical to the stability and growth of the financial system and the economy as a whole.

2.20 Can you describe the basic structure of a financial statement, and what information it provides?

A financial statement is a document that shows the financial performance and position of a company over a period of time. The basic structure of a financial statement consists of four parts: the balance sheet, the income statement, the cash flow statement, and the statement of equity.

The balance sheet shows the assets, liabilities, and equity of the company at a specific point in time. It is divided into two sections: assets and liabilities & equity. The assets section shows what the company owns or controls, such as cash, investments, property, and inventory. The liabilities & equity section shows what the company owes, such as debts to creditors and shareholders' equity.

The income statement shows the revenues, expenses, and profits of the company over a period of time, such as a quarter or year. It starts with the company's revenue and subtracts the cost of goods sold and other expenses to arrive at net income. This statement helps investors understand the financial performance of the company, including how much money it is making and where that money is going.

The cash flow statement shows how the company's cash balance changed over a period of time. It is broken down into three parts: operating activities, investing activities, and financing activities. Operating activities include the cash flows related to the company's primary operations, such as sales and production. Investing activities include the cash flows related to investments in property, plant and equipment, and other long-term assets. Financing activities include the cash flows related to financing the company's operations, such as issuing or repurchasing stock or taking out loans.

The statement of equity shows the changes in shareholder equity over a period of time. It starts with the beginning balance of shareholder equity, adds any investments or contributions made by shareholders, subtracts any distributions or dividends paid to shareholders, and adjusts for any changes in the value of equity, such as stock repurchases or changes in accounting principles.

Together, these four financial statements provide a complete picture of a company's financial performance and position, allowing investors to make informed decisions about whether to invest in a company or not.

Chapter 3

Intermediate

3.1 What is the main difference between a call option and a put option, and how do they work?

A call option and a put option are two types of options commonly used in financial markets. The key difference between them lies in the right they each offer to the buyer: a call option gives the buyer the right (but not the obligation) to buy an underlying asset at a specified price (the strike price), while a put option gives the buyer the right (but not the obligation) to sell an underlying asset at a specified price (the strike price).

In more detail, a call option grants the buyer the right to purchase the underlying asset at the specified strike price before the option expires. The seller of the call option (also known as the writer) agrees to sell the asset to the buyer at the strike price if the buyer chooses to exercise their right. The buyer of a call option hopes that the price of the underlying asset will increase above the strike price so that they can profit from the trade.

On the other hand, a put option gives the buyer the right to sell an underlying asset at the specified strike price before the option expires. The writer of the put option agrees to buy the asset from the buyer at the strike price if the buyer chooses to exercise their right. The buyer of the put option hopes that the price of the underlying asset will decrease below the strike price so that they can profit from the trade.

To illustrate, let's consider an example where an investor buys a call option on the stock of company ABC with a strike price of \$50 and an expiration date in one month. If the current market price of ABC stock is \$45 and it increases to \$55 before the expiration date, the investor can exercise their right to buy the stock for \$50 and then sell it at the current market price of \$55, making a profit of \$5 per share. Meanwhile, if the stock price remains below \$50, the investor does not have to exercise the option and simply lets it expire, losing only the price of the option premium.

For a further example, consider an investor who buys a put option on the same stock of company ABC with a strike price of \$50 and one-month expiry. If the stock price declines to \$45 before the expiry, the investor can then exercise the put option to sell the stock at the agreed strike price of \$50, making a profit of \$5 per share. However, if the stock price rises above \$50, the investor will not exercise the option and simply let it expire, losing only the price of the option premium.

In summary, call and put options offer investors the opportunity to profit from potential price movements in the underlying assets, while also offering downside protection in the form of limiting potential losses to the premium paid for the option.

3.2   How do you calculate the duration and convexity of a bond, and why are they important?

Duration and convexity are two important measures of bond price sensitivity to changes in interest rates.

Duration represents the average time it takes to receive the bond's cash flows. Mathematically, duration is the weighted average of the times over which the cash flows occur, where the weights are the present values of the cash flows. The formula for Macaulay duration is as follows:

$$D = \frac{\sum_{t=1}^{T} t \times CF_t}{P}$$

where D is the Macaulay duration of the bond, CF_t is the cash flow at time t, T is the bond's maturity, and P is the bond's price.

Convexity measures how the duration of the bond changes as interest rates change. Specifically, it measures the curvature of the relationship between the bond price and the yield. Convexity can be defined as the rate of change of duration with respect to yield. The formula for convexity is as follows:

$$C = \frac{\sum_{t=1}^{T} \frac{t(t+1)}{2} \times CF_t}{P \times (1+y)^2}$$

where C is the convexity of the bond, CF_t and T are as defined in the duration formula, and y is the yield to maturity of the bond.

Duration and convexity are important because they help bond investors and analysts to understand how a bond's price is likely to react to changes in interest rates. Specifically, bonds with higher duration and convexity are more sensitive to changes in interest rates, while bonds with lower duration and convexity are less sensitive. This information can be used to construct bond portfolios that are more or less sensitive to interest rate changes, depending on the investor's risk tolerance and investment objectives.

For example, suppose an investor is considering two bonds: Bond A has a duration of 5 years and convexity of 20, while Bond B has a duration of 10 years and convexity of 50. If interest rates rise by 1%, the price of Bond A would be expected to fall by approximately 5%, while the price of Bond B would be expected to fall by approximately 10%. This means that Bond B is more sensitive to interest rate changes than Bond A. If the investor is interested in preserving capital and avoiding losses due to interest rate changes, they may choose to invest in Bond A instead of Bond B. Conversely, if the investor is willing to take on more risk in exchange for potential higher returns, they may choose to invest in Bond B.

3.3   Can you explain the concept of hedging and provide an example of a hedging strategy?

Hedging is a risk management technique used to offset potential losses in a particular investment by taking an opposite position in a related market. The idea is to reduce or eliminate the exposure to the risk of an asset's price movement by taking a position in a related asset that tends to move in the opposite direction.

Hedging can be done in various ways such as options, futures, swaps, forwards, and diversification. A well-designed hedging strategy can protect investors' portfolios from significant losses in a volatile market.

Here is an example of a hedging strategy using futures contracts:

Suppose that an investor owns a portfolio of stocks that represent the S&P 500 index, and she is concerned that the market might decline over the next few months. To hedge this portfolio, the investor may decide to sell futures contracts.

Each futures contract represents an agreement to buy or sell an underlying asset at a predetermined price at a specific time in the future. In this case, the futures contracts are based on the S&P 500 index.

If the S&P 500 index declines, the value of the futures contracts will increase, offsetting some of the losses in the stock portfolio. Conversely, if the S&P 500 index increases, the value of the futures contracts will decrease, but the stocks in the portfolio will gain in value.

For example, suppose that an investor owns a $1 million portfolio of S&P 500 stocks and sells three futures contracts on the S&P 500 index, each with a notional value of $250,000. If the S&P 500 index declines by 10%, the value of the stocks in the portfolio would decrease by $100,000 ($1 million x 10%). However, the value of the futures contracts would increase by $75,000 (3 x $250,000 x 0.10). The net loss on the portfolio would be reduced to $25,000.

Overall, hedging can help investors protect their portfolios against unwanted risks and minimize potential losses.

3.4   What is the role of interest rates in the valuation of financial assets?

Interest rates play a crucial role in the valuation of financial assets. This is because the value of a financial asset is fundamentally based on the future expected cash flows it will generate, and interest rates are one of the primary determinants of the present value of those cash flows.

To explain this concept more formally, we can use the concept of present value (PV), which is the current value of a future stream of cash flows that will be received at various times in the future. The formula for calculating the present value of a cash flow (CF) received at time t in the future is:

$$PV = CF/(1+r)^t$$

where r is the discount rate, or the interest rate used to determine the present value of the cash flow. The higher the discount rate, the lower the present value of the cash flow.

Using this formula, we can see that interest rates play a critical role in the valuation of financial assets. Bond prices, for example, are highly sensitive to changes in interest rates because the cash flows generated by a bond are fixed and known in advance, and the bond's value is the present value of those cash flows. As interest rates rise, the discount rate used to calculate the present value of those cash flows also rises, leading to a lower bond price. Conversely, when interest rates fall, the discount rate used to calculate the present value of those cash flows also falls, leading to a higher bond price.

Similarly, the valuation of stocks can also be affected by interest rates. While the cash flows generated by a stock are not fixed like a bond, the present value of those cash flows is still sensitive to changes in interest rates. This is because the risk-free rate, which is often used as a benchmark for discounting the future cash flows of a stock, is itself based on the prevailing interest rates in the economy. As interest rates rise, the risk-free rate also rises, leading to a lower present value of future cash flows and a lower stock price. Conversely, when interest rates fall, the risk-free rate also falls, leading to a higher present value of future cash flows and a higher stock price.

In conclusion, interest rates are a critical component of the valuation of financial assets. Changes in interest rates can have a significant impact on the present value of future cash flows generated by financial assets, which in turn affects their market value. As such, investors should always monitor interest rates and their likely direction when making investment decisions.

3.5 Can you describe the process of arbitrage and how it contributes to market efficiency?

Arbitrage is the process of exploiting price differences of identical or similar financial instruments across different markets. The aim of an arbitrageur is to make riskless profits by buying low in one market and selling high in another market, taking advantage of price discrepancies.

The concept of arbitrage is based on the efficiency of the market. If a financial instrument is mispriced due to any reason such as inefficient information dissemination or human emotions, an arbitrageur can profit by correcting the price discrepancy. This process of profit-making attracts other traders to buy or sell the instrument, leading to an increased demand/supply, and eventually, the price discrepancy is corrected. Thus, arbitrage contributes to the efficient pricing of assets in the market.

There are several types of arbitrage such as:

1. Spatial arbitrage: This is a type of arbitrage where an asset is bought in one location and sold in another location where the price is higher. For example, if crude oil is priced lower in one country than in another, a trader could buy crude oil in the cheaper country and sell it in the more expensive country, making a profit on the price difference.

2. Temporal arbitrage: This is a type of arbitrage where an asset is bought at a lower price and sold at a higher price in the same market but at different times. For example, if an investor expects the price of a stock to increase in the future, he could buy the stock now and sell it later for a profit.

3. Statistical arbitrage: This is a type of arbitrage where trading strategies are developed based on the statistical analysis of price movements and correlations between financial instruments.

The presence of arbitrage opportunities in the market contributes to price efficiency since traders would buy or sell assets to correct price discrepancies. As a result, arbitrage helps to ensure that assets are priced fairly in the market, which is critical for maintaining investor confidence and market stability. However, it is important to note that arbitrage opportunities are often short-lived, given that traders would quickly take advantage of them, which would correct the price discrepancy.

3.6 What are the main types of quantitative models used in finance, and what are their key applications?

There are several types of quantitative models used in finance, and they serve different purposes. Some of the main types are:

1. Black-Scholes model: This model is used to determine the price of European-style stock options. It assumes that stock prices follow a geometric Brownian motion and that options can be continuously traded. The Black-Scholes model is widely used in finance for pricing options and has numerous applications, such as valuing employee stock options and creating structured products.

$$C = S_0 N(d_1) - Ke^{-rT} N(d_2)$$

where C is the call option price, S_0 is the stock price, K is the
exercise price, r is the risk-free interest rate, T is the time to
maturity, and $N(d)$ is the cumulative distribution function of
the standard normal distribution, with:

$$d_1 = \frac{ln(\frac{S_0}{K}) + (r + \frac{\sigma^2}{2})T}{\sigma\sqrt{T}}$$

and

$$d_2 = d_1 - \sigma\sqrt{T}$$

2. Vasicek model: This model is used to model the interest
rate process, and it assumes that interest rates follow a mean-
reverting process. The Vasicek model is commonly used in bond
pricing and interest rate derivative pricing.

$$dr_t = a(b - r_t)dt + \sigma dW_t$$

where r_t is the interest rate at time t, a is the rate of mean reversion, b is the long-term mean interest rate, σ is the volatility
of the interest rate process, and dW_t is a Brownian motion.

3. Value-at-Risk (VaR) model: This model is used to estimate
the potential losses on a portfolio over a given time period with
a specified level of confidence. VaR is widely used in risk management to quantify and manage market risk.

4. Monte Carlo simulation: This model is used to generate data
by simulating random events. This technique is widely used in

finance for option pricing, risk management, and investment analysis.

```
# Example of Monte Carlo simulation in option pricing
import math
import numpy as np

# Define input parameters
S0 = 100 # initial stock price
K = 105 # strike price
T = 1.0 # time to maturity
r = 0.05 # risk-free interest rate
sigma = 0.2 # volatility

# Define the number of simulations
n_sim = 100000

# Generate simulated stock prices
Z = np.random.standard_normal(n_sim)
ST = S0 * np.exp((r - 0.5 * sigma**2) * T + sigma * math.sqrt(T) * Z
    )

# Calculate option payoff
hT = np.maximum(ST - K, 0)

# Calculate option price
C0 = math.exp(-r * T) * np.mean(hT)

print("Option price =", C0)
```

3.7   How do you calculate Value at Risk (VaR) for a portfolio, and why is it important?

Value at Risk (VaR) is a measure of the maximum potential loss that a portfolio could suffer within a given time period, at a certain level of confidence. It is an important tool used by risk managers to measure and manage market risk. VaR tells us how much we could expect to lose (in dollar or percentage terms) with a given probability over a certain time horizon.

There are different VaR approaches to calculate the potential

loss of a portfolio. The most common ones are historical simulation, variance-covariance (or parametric) method, and Monte
Carlo simulation.

Historical Simulation: This method uses historical prices to
calculate the potential loss of a portfolio. It assumes that the
future price movements will be similar to the ones that have
occurred in the past. The steps to calculate VaR using historical
simulation method are:

1. Sort historical returns in increasing order

2. Select the worst "x" percent of returns which represents the level
of confidence of the VaR calculation

3. The loss is then computed as the negative of the return at that
level.

The formula for historical VaR is:

$$VaR_\alpha = -F_\alpha^{-1}(R_p)$$

where F_α^{-1} is the inverse cumulative distribution function of the
portfolio return distribution and R_p is the portfolio return.

Variance-Covariance Method: This method uses the normal distribution assumption for portfolio returns. It calculates the
standard deviation of the portfolio returns and the correlation
structure between the assets in the portfolio. The formula for
variance-covariance VaR is:

$$VaR_\alpha = \sqrt{w'\Sigma w}F_\alpha^{-1}(Z)$$

where w is the vector of asset weights in the portfolio, Σ is the
covariance matrix of asset returns, $F_\alpha^{-1}(Z)$ is the inverse cumulative distribution function of the standard normal distribution
and Z is the one-tailed confidence level.

Monte Carlo Simulation: This method generates random scenarios of asset returns based on their statistical distribution. The portfolio value is then re-computed for each scenario, and VaR is determined from the distribution of the simulated portfolio returns. The formula for Monte Carlo VaR is:

$$VaR_\alpha = -F_\alpha^{-1}(R_p)$$

where R_p is the distribution of simulated portfolio returns and F_α^{-1} is the inverse cumulative distribution function of the portfolio return distribution.

VaR is important because it provides information on how much the portfolio could lose over a given time period, which helps to set risk limits, allocate capital to trading desks, and evaluate the adequacy of a firm's capital. VaR can also be used to compare alternative investment strategies, assess the performance of a portfolio manager, and serve as a basis for regulatory capital requirements. However, it is important to note that VaR has limitations as it assumes that the underlying statistical distribution of returns is known and that it does not consider tail risk, i.e., the potential for extreme losses beyond what is captured by the VaR calculation.

3.8   What is the main purpose of Monte Carlo simulation in quantitative finance?

Monte Carlo simulation is a powerful tool in quantitative finance used to estimate the probability distribution of potential outcomes by running multiple scenarios with random variables. Its main purpose is to value complex financial derivatives, sim-

ulate stock prices, and build an understanding of risk in portfolios.

In finance, many market factors that influence prices and returns cannot be consistently described by known probability
distributions. For example, the behavior of stock prices and
exchange rates can be unpredictable, as they are influenced by
many unforeseeable factors such as political events, major economic developments, and natural disasters. When these market
factors are uncertain or when the information is incomplete or
contested, Monte Carlo simulation can be used to estimate the
potential range of outcomes.

In general, to perform Monte Carlo simulation, the analyst se-
lects a starting point, or initial conditions, for each variable
and then repeatedly runs simulations, adjusting the values of
the input parameters at each iteration. The simulation calculates a value for each trial, allowing the analyst to construct
a probability distribution of possible outcomes. Monte Carlo
simulation can be performed with simple simulations, such as
coin-flipping experiments, or with complex stochastic models,
like the Black-Scholes options pricing formula.

In quantitative finance, one of the most common applications of
Monte Carlo simulation is in options pricing. The Black-Scholes
formula assumes that the price of the underlying asset follows
an approximately normal, or log-normal, distribution, but this
assumption can be problematic. Monte Carlo simulation can
be used to estimate the probability distribution of the option's
price by simulating future stock prices and calculating the option price for each simulated stock price. Another important
application of Monte Carlo simulation is in risk management.
Monte Carlo simulation can help quantify the level of risk in a
portfolio by simulating the potential returns of each asset in the

portfolio and calculating the expected value of the portfolio.

In conclusion, Monte Carlo simulation is a crucial tool in quantitative finance for estimating the probability distribution of financial outcomes, valuing complex financial instruments, and assessing portfolio risk. It is an essential technique for analyzing and predicting financial outcomes in an uncertain world.

3.9   How do you perform a sensitivity analysis, and what is its purpose in financial modeling?

Performing a sensitivity analysis is an important step in financial modeling, which aims to assess the impact of changes in inputs or assumptions on the model outputs. Sensitivity analysis helps to identify the most significant drivers of the model and understand how changes in them can affect the outcomes. It also helps in assessing the model's reliability by exploring the range of possible outcomes under various scenarios.

The process of performing a sensitivity analysis involves the following steps:

1. Determine the inputs - Identify the input parameters used in the model that may have a significant impact on the results. For example, in a discounted cash flow (DCF) valuation model, the inputs could include revenue growth rate, discount rate, terminal value, etc.

2. Define the ranges - Define a range of values for each input parameter. This range could be based on historical data, expert

judgment, or industry benchmarks.

3. Run the model - Run the model for each combination of input parameter values. This could be done manually or through simulation software that automates the process.

4. Analyze the results - Evaluate the impact of changes in input parameters on the model output. Identify the most influential drivers of the model and understand how changes in them affect the outcome.

5. Interpret the results - Interpret the results to draw conclusions and make decisions. For example, if a small change in the discount rate leads to a significant change in the valuation, it may indicate that the company's future cash flows are highly dependent on the cost of capital.

In financial modeling, sensitivity analysis plays a vital role in decision-making by helping stakeholders to evaluate the robustness and reliability of the model. For example, a sensitivity analysis of a project's financial model can help management to assess how changing cost or revenue assumptions may impact future profits. Similarly, a sensitivity analysis in a risk model can help investors to understand how changes in market conditions can affect the portfolio's value.

Here is an example of a sensitivity analysis in a DCF model:

Assume we are valuing a startup using a DCF model based on projected cash flow for the next five years. The company has an estimated free cash flow of \$100,000 per year, and we assume a discount rate of 12%. We want to perform a sensitivity analysis to understand the impact of changes in the discount rate on the enterprise value (EV).

Our sensitivity analysis could involve the following steps:

1. Determine the inputs - The input parameters are free cash flow and discount rate.

2. Define the ranges - We could vary the discount rate from 10% to 15% in increments of 0.5%.

3. Run the model - We could calculate the enterprise value for each combination of free cash flow and discount rate.

4. Analyze the results - We could plot the enterprise value against the discount rate for each free cash flow scenario. The resulting graph would show the impact of changes in the discount rate on the enterprise value.

5. Interpret the results - We would use the sensitivity analysis to determine the range of possible enterprise values for different discount rates. If the range is significant, management may need to reconsider their assumptions or make changes to their business plan to reduce risk and uncertainty.

3.10   Can you explain the concept of volatility in finance and how it is measured?

Volatility is a measurement of the degree of fluctuation of an asset's price over a specific period of time. Financial analysts and investors use volatility as an essential metric to understand the potential for risk and expected returns of an asset.

Volatility can be measured in multiple ways, including measuring historical price movements, implied volatility from options market prices, and evaluating future volatility using quantitative methods. In finance, volatility is often measured using standard deviation, which gives the degree of variation of prices from their mean or average price over a specific time period.

The standard deviation of an asset's price returns can be calculated as follows:

$$\sigma = \sqrt{\frac{1}{n-1}\sum_{i=1}^{n}(r_i - \bar{r})^2} \qquad (3.1)$$

where σ is the standard deviation, n is the total number of returns, r_i is the return at a specific time i, and $\bar{r}$ is the mean return.

High volatility indicates that an asset's price moves more rapidly over a given period, suggesting that the asset price could potentially experience large price swings in the future. On the other hand, low volatility suggests a more stable asset price, indicating less potential for dramatic price swings.

For instance, consider two stocks A and B. Stock A has an average daily price increase of 1%, with a standard deviation of 0.5%. In contrast, stock B has an average daily price increase of 1%, with a standard deviation of 1.5%.

Although both stocks have the same average daily price increase, stock B is significantly more volatile due to a higher standard deviation. This suggests that stock B's price is more likely to fluctuate significantly compared to stock A's price.

By measuring volatility, investors can make more informed decisions about their investment strategy. If an investor can tolerate higher volatility, they might consider investing in more volatile assets with the potential for higher returns. Conversely, investors with a lower risk tolerance might choose less volatile assets with more stable price movements.

3.11   What is a yield curve, and what information does it provide to investors?

A yield curve is a graphical representation of the relationship between the interest rate and the time to maturity of a fixed income security such as a bond. The yield curve is constructed by plotting the yields (or interest rates) of bonds with different maturities against those maturities. Generally, the yield curve is upward sloping, indicating that bonds with longer maturities have higher yields than those with shorter maturities.

The yield curve provides important information to investors regarding the future direction of interest rates and the state of the economy. In particular, the slope of the yield curve and the steepness of its slope are often used as indicators of future economic growth and inflation. A steep upward sloping yield curve, for instance, implies that investors expect economic growth and inflation to accelerate in the future. Conversely, a flat or inverted yield curve suggests that investors are bullish on short-term bonds and expect interest rates to remain relatively low, which is often an indication of a possible recession or a slow economy.

Investors can use the yield curve to determine which bonds to purchase based on their investment objectives and market expectations. For example, an investor who is bullish on economic

growth and expects interest rates to rise in the future may consider purchasing long-term bonds to lock in higher yields before
bond prices fall. In contrast, an investor who believes there is
a risk of a recession is likely to consider purchasing short-term
bonds or cash equivalents to protect their portfolio from potential losses.

In addition, the yield curve also provides information about
the relative pricing of different types of bonds with different
maturities. For example, if a bond with a 10-year maturity has a
higher yield than a bond with a 1-year maturity, it suggests that
investors perceive greater risk in holding the longer-term bond,
which may result in a higher coupon rate to compensate for
that risk. By analyzing the yield curve, investors can compare
the relative value of bonds with different maturities and make
appropriate investment decisions.

3.12   What is the difference between co-variance and correlation in finance, and how are they used in portfolio management?

Covariance and correlation are two important statistical concepts commonly used in finance and portfolio management.
Both covariance and correlation measures the degree to which
two variables are related to each other, but they have different
interpretations and uses in financial analysis.

Covariance is a measure of how much two variables move together. It is defined as the expected value of the product of the
deviations of two random variables from their respective means:

$$\text{Cov}(X, Y) = E[(X - E[X])(Y - E[Y])]$$

If the covariance is positive, it means that the two variables tend to move in the same direction. If the covariance is negative, it means that they tend to move in opposite directions. However, the magnitude of the covariance is not standardized, so it is difficult to compare covariances across different datasets.

Correlation, on the other hand, is a standardized measure of the relationship between two variables. It is defined as the covariance of the two variables divided by the product of their standard deviations:

$$\rho_{X,Y} = \frac{\text{Cov}(X, Y)}{\sigma_X \sigma_Y}$$

where σ_X and σ_Y are the standard deviations of X and Y, respectively. Correlation is always between -1 and 1; a correlation of 1 means that the two variable move perfectly in the same direction, a correlation of -1 means they move perfectly in opposite directions, and a correlation of 0 means there is no relationship between the two variables.

In finance, both covariance and correlation are used in portfolio management to help investors diversify their holdings. The goal of diversification is to mix different assets in a way that reduces overall risk while maintaining a desired level of return. Covariance is used to calculate the variance of a portfolio, which is a measure of how much the returns of the assets in the portfolio fluctuate around the expected return of the portfolio. A portfolio that contains assets with high covariance will have higher variance, and therefore higher risk, than a portfolio that contains assets with low covariance.

Correlation is used to determine which assets should be included in a portfolio to reduce the overall risk. Diversification is most effective when assets with low or negative correlation are combined. Assets that are highly correlated, on the other hand, will tend to move together, so including multiple highly correlated assets in a portfolio provides little diversification benefit.

In summary, covariance measures the degree to which two variables move together, while correlation is a standardized measure of the relationship between two variables. Both are important in portfolio management, with covariance used to calculate portfolio variance and correlation used to determine which assets should be included in a portfolio to reduce overall risk.

3.13   How does the binomial option pricing model work, and how does it differ from the Black-Scholes model?

The binomial option pricing model is a method to price options by assuming that the underlying asset can move up or down by a certain percentage at each time step until the expiration date. The model is based on the assumption that the options can only be exercised at expiration. It is a discrete-time model that involves building a binary tree representing all the possible price movements of the underlying asset until the expiration date.

To value an option using the binomial model, the first step is to construct the binomial tree. The tree has a set number of levels representing the different expiration dates for the option and a set number of possible price movements at each level. The probability of the stock going up or down is calculated using the volatility of the stock and the time interval between each node in the tree. Once the binomial tree is constructed, the option value can be calculated by working backwards through the tree from the final expiration date, calculating the expected value at each node at each level.

The Black-Scholes model, on the other hand, is a continuous-time model that assumes the underlying asset has a random walk with constant volatility, and that the option can be exercised at any time before the expiration date. The model uses the concept of a risk-neutral probability measure to value the option. The key formulas used in the Black-Scholes model are:

$$\frac{\partial C}{\partial t} + \frac{1}{2}\sigma^2 S^2 \frac{\partial^2 C}{\partial S^2} + rS\frac{\partial C}{\partial S} - rC = 0$$

where C is the price of the call option, S is the price of the underlying asset, σ^2 is the volatility of the underlying asset, r is the risk-free interest rate, and t is time.

The Black-Scholes model assumes that the underlying asset follows a log-normal distribution of prices and that the option can be exercised at any time before expiration. The model requires the input of five variables: the underlying asset price, the strike price, the time to expiration, the risk-free interest rate, and the volatility of the underlying asset.

One of the main differences between the binomial option pricing model and the Black-Scholes model is that the binomial model assumes that the underlying asset can only move up or down, while the Black-Scholes model assumes a continuous range of stock price movements. Another major difference is that the binomial model works well for American options, which can be exercised at any time before expiration, while the Black-Scholes model is mostly used for European options, which can only be exercised at expiration. Finally, the Black-Scholes model is a closed-form solution, meaning that it can be solved using a simple formula, while the binomial model requires a computationally intensive tree-building process.

3.14   What are the main components of the GARCH model, and how is it used to model volatility?

The Generalized Autoregressive Conditional Heteroscedasticity (GARCH) model is a popular econometric time series model used to model and forecast volatility in financial markets. It was proposed by Robert Engle in 1982 and is an extension of the Autoregressive Conditional Heteroscedasticity (ARCH) model.

The GARCH model has three main components:

1. The mean equation: This is used to model the expected return of the asset. It is typically represented as an autoregressive or moving average model. For example, a simple AR(1) mean equation can be written as:

$$y_t = \phi_0 + \phi_1 y_{t-1} + \varepsilon_t$$

where y_t is the asset return at time t, ϕ_0 and ϕ_1 are parameters to be estimated, and ε_t is the error term.

2. The volatility equation: This is used to model the conditional variance of the asset return, which is assumed to be time-varying. The GARCH model assumes that the volatility is a function of past squared errors or shocks. For example, a simple GARCH(1,1) volatility equation can be written as:

$$\sigma_t^2 = \omega + \alpha_1 \varepsilon_{t-1}^2 + \beta_1 \sigma_{t-1}^2$$

where σ_t^2 is the conditional variance at time t, ω is a constant term, α_1 and β_1 are parameters to be estimated, ε_{t-1}^2 is the squared error term at time t-1 and σ_{t-1}^2 is the conditional variance at time t-1.

3. The error term: This is assumed to be normally distributed with zero mean and constant variance.

The GARCH model is used to model volatility by estimating the parameters of the mean and volatility equations and then using the model to forecast future volatility. The model assumes that volatility is persistent, meaning that past shocks have a long-lasting effect on the current volatility. This persistence is captured through the use of the lagged squared error term in the volatility equation.

One common application of the GARCH model is in Option pricing, where volatility plays a key role in determining the value of the Option. The GARCH model can help model the volatility of the underlying asset and thus can aid in pricing Options more accurately.

Another application is in risk management, where traders and financial institutions use the model to compute Value at Risk (VaR) and Expected Shortfall (ES) metrics, which are critical in assessing the likelihood of large losses in the event of an adverse market move.

Overall, the GARCH model is a useful tool for analyzing and forecasting financial market volatility, and it has been extensively used in research and industry.

3.15 Can you explain the concept of liquidity risk, and how can it be mitigated?

Liquidity risk can be defined as the risk of not being able to trade an asset or a security in the market without incurring significant transaction costs or price discounts due to lack of buyers or sellers, or a breakdown in the normal market mechanisms. In other words, it is the risk of not being able to convert an asset into cash quickly and at a fair price when needed, which can impact the ability of an individual or an organization to meet their financial obligations or fund their operations.

Liquidity risk can arise due to various reasons, such as changes in market conditions, sudden demand for liquidity, credit events, regulatory changes, operational issues, or other unforeseen events. It can affect all types of assets and securities, including stocks, bonds, currencies, commodities, derivatives, and structured products.

Mitigating liquidity risk involves ensuring that there is sufficient market depth and liquidity in the assets and securities held by an individual or an organization, as well as having a robust risk management framework to identify, monitor, and manage liquidity risks. The following are some of the measures that can be taken to mitigate liquidity risk:

1. Diversification: By investing in a diversified range of assets and securities across different asset classes, geographies, and sectors, an individual or an organization can reduce the concentration risk and the impact of any single asset or security on overall liquidity.

2. Asset Liability Management: By matching the maturity and liquidity profile of assets and liabilities, an individual or an organization can ensure that they have sufficient cash flows to meet their obligations when they fall due.

3. Stress Testing: By conduct stress tests that simulate adverse market conditions or events and assess their impact on the liquidity of the portfolio, an individual or an organization can identify potential vulnerabilities and take proactive measures to address them.

4. Contingency Planning: By having contingency plans in place to access emergency funding sources, such as credit lines or other forms of backup liquidity, an individual or an organization can have a safety net to fall back on in case of unforeseen events.

5. Monitoring and Reporting: By regularly monitoring their liquidity positions and reporting to senior management and other stakeholders, an individual or an organization can ensure that they are aware of their liquidity risks and can take timely corrective actions if needed.

In summary, liquidity risk is an important aspect of financial

risk management, and it can be mitigated through a combination of portfolio diversification, asset liability management,
stress testing, contingency planning, and monitoring and reporting.

3.16   What are the main types of credit risk, and how can they be assessed?

Credit risk is defined as the potential loss that an investor may
suffer due to the inability of a borrower to make payments on
a debt obligation. There are various types of credit risk, and
I will describe some of the main types and how they can be
assessed.

1. Sovereign Risk: Sovereign risk is the risk that a government
can't meet its debt obligations. It is assessed by looking at the
credit rating of a country, and factors such as economic growth,
inflation, and political stability. For example, a country with a
high credit rating and stable economic and political conditions
is considered to have lower sovereign risk.

2. Counterparty Risk: Counterparty risk is the risk that a
borrower is unable to repay its debt obligation to the lender.
This risk can be assessed by looking at the creditworthiness
of the borrower, such as its credit rating, financial statements,
and management team. For example, a borrower with a high
credit rating, strong financials, and experienced management
team may be deemed to have lower counterparty risk.

3. Industry Risk: Industry risk refers to the risk that a particular industry is facing challenges or experiencing a downturn,
which could impact the borrower's ability to repay its debt obli-

gations. Industry risk can be assessed by analyzing macroeconomic factors such as interest rates, unemployment rates, and economic growth, as well as industry-specific factors such as competition, market demand, and regulatory changes.

4. Concentration Risk: Concentration risk is the risk that a lender has too much exposure to a particular counterparty, industry or a geographic region. It can be assessed by analyzing the lender's portfolio diversification, and assessing the potential impact of a default or downturn on the overall portfolio.

5. Credit Migration Risk: Credit migration risk is the risk that a borrower's credit rating will deteriorate over time, leading to potential defaults. Credit migration risk can be assessed by analyzing historical default rates and by using quantitative models to predict the probability of a borrower's credit rating downgrade.

Overall, assessing credit risk involves analyzing a range of qualitative and quantitative factors, including credit ratings, financial statements, industry-specific factors, macroeconomic conditions, and portfolio diversification. It is important to note that credit risk cannot be completely eliminated, but can be managed and mitigated through prudent risk management practices.

3.17   How do you calculate the Sharpe ratio for a portfolio, and what does it indicate?

The Sharpe ratio is a widely used measure of risk-adjusted return in finance. It was introduced by William F. Sharpe in 1966, and it measures how much excess return an investor can obtain per unit of risk taken on an investment.

Mathematically, the Sharpe ratio is defined as the ratio of the excess return of a portfolio over the risk-free rate (typically the rate of return on a government bond) to the standard deviation of that excess return: ·

$$Sharpe\ Ratio = \frac{R_p - R_f}{\sigma_p}$$

where,

R_p is the portfolio's average annual return over a certain period,

R_f is the risk-free rate of return over the same period,

σ_p is the portfolio's standard deviation.

The Sharpe ratio calculation provides a way to measure the risk-adjusted performance of a portfolio. The higher the Sharpe ratio, the better the portfolio's risk-adjusted return. A Sharpe ratio of 1 or more is generally considered good, while a ratio below 1 may indicate that the portfolio is not generating enough excess return to justify the risk taken on.

For example, suppose that a portfolio has an average annual

return of 10% and a standard deviation of 12%, while the risk-free rate of return for the same period is 2%. The Sharpe ratio for this portfolio would be:

$$Sharpe\ Ratio = \frac{10\% - 2\%}{12\%} = 0.667$$

This means that for each unit of risk taken on by the portfolio, the excess return generated is equal to 0.667 units.

In practice, it is important to consider the drawbacks of the Sharpe ratio. For instance, it assumes that returns are normally distributed and that the investor's utility function is represented by a quadratic function of the returns. In addition, the Sharpe ratio can be sensitive to outliers and to the choice of the risk-free rate. Nevertheless, it remains a valuable tool for comparing the risk-adjusted performance of different portfolios or investment strategies.

3.18   Can you explain the role of alpha and beta in portfolio management?

In portfolio management, the concept of alpha and beta is widely used to measure and control portfolio risk and return.

Beta measures the systematic risk of a portfolio or security compared to the market. It indicates the sensitivity of the portfolio or security to changes in the market. A beta of 1 means that the portfolio or security moves in line with the market; a beta less than 1 means that the portfolio or security is less volatile than the market, and a beta greater than 1 means that the portfolio or security is more volatile than the market.

In mathematical terms, beta is defined as:

$$\beta = \frac{\text{Cov}(r_p, r_m)}{\text{Var}(r_m)}$$

Where:

r_p is the portfolio return

r_m is the market return

Cov is the covariance

Var is the variance

Alpha, on the other hand, measures the excess return of a portfolio or security relative to a benchmark like the market. It represents the value added by the investment manager through his/her selection and timing decisions.

In mathematical terms, alpha can be defined as:

$$\alpha = r_p - (r_f + \beta(r_m - r_f))$$

where:

r_f is the risk-free rate of return

r_m is the market return

β is the systematic risk factor

r_p is the portfolio return

Thus, in portfolio management, a portfolio manager tries to achieve higher alpha by selecting stocks or securities that will outperform the market, while incorporating diversification strategies to minimize beta and hence systemic risk.

For example, if the market is expected to go up, a portfolio manager can select stocks with high beta, to take advantage of the market movement. Similarly, if the market is expected to go down, the portfolio manager can select stocks with low beta to protect the portfolio from the market downside.

Overall, alpha and beta play crucial roles in portfolio management by helping portfolio managers to measure and control portfolio risk and return.

3.19   What are the main differences between a forward contract and a futures contract?

A forward contract is a private agreement between two parties to buy or sell an asset at a future date and at a specified price. The terms of the forward contract are determined by the parties involved in the contract, and they are not standardized. The lack of standardization of forward contracts means that they are not traded on exchanges and are not fungible.

On the other hand, a futures contract is a standardized contract that is traded on an exchange, and it obligates the buyer or seller to buy or sell an underlying asset at a future date and at

a specified price. The terms of futures contracts are determined
by the exchange where they are traded, and they are subject to
daily margin requirements.

The main differences between forward and futures contracts are
as follows:

1. Standardization: Futures contracts are standardized, which
makes them fungible and tradable on exchanges. Forward contracts are not standardized, which makes them less liquid.

2. Counterparty risk: In a forward contract, there is a risk that
one of the parties may default on their obligations. In a futures
contract, the exchange acts as a counterparty to both parties,
which eliminates this risk.

3. Margin requirements: Futures contracts require daily margin payments to be made by both parties to ensure that they
fulfill their obligations. Forward contracts do not have margin
requirements.

4. Settlement: Futures contracts are settled daily through a
clearinghouse, which ensures that both parties fulfill their obligations. Forward contracts are settled on the maturity date.

5. Cost: Futures contracts generally have a lower cost than
forward contracts because of the competition among market
participants on the exchange.

In summary, while both forward and futures contracts are agreements to buy or sell an asset at a future date and at a specified price, the main differences include standardization, counterparty risk, margin requirements, settlement and cost.

3.20 Can you describe the process of bootstrapping in the context of yield curve construction?

In the context of yield curve construction, bootstrapping refers to a technique used to determine the zero-coupon yield curve that is consistent with a given set of bond prices. The basic idea behind the technique is to start with the closest bond maturity available and use its price to estimate the zero-coupon yield at that maturity. Then, this yield is used to calculate the present value of the bond cash flows, and the resulting present value is subtracted from the bond price to obtain the value of the residual cash flow. This process is repeated for all the other available bonds, and the resulting set of residual cash flows provides the information needed to estimate the zero-coupon yields at the remaining maturities.

To illustrate the process more formally, suppose we have a set of n coupon-bearing bonds with maturities T1, T2, ..., Tn and coupon rates C1, C2, ..., Cn, and suppose that the market prices of these bonds are P1, P2, ..., Pn, respectively. The goal is to estimate the zero-coupon yield curve at maturities T1, T2, ..., Tn. The first step is to estimate the zero-coupon yield at the shortest maturity, T1. This can be done by solving the following equation for y1:

$$P_1 = \frac{C_1}{1 + y_1} + \frac{C_1}{(1 + y_1)^2} + ... + \frac{C_1}{(1 + y_1)^{T_1 - 1}} + \frac{1}{(1 + y_1)^{T_1}}$$

Once y1 is determined, it can be used to estimate the value of the residual cash flow for the second bond, which is given by:

$$R_2 = P_2 - \frac{C_2}{(1+y_1)} - \frac{C_2}{(1+y_1)^2} - \cdots - \frac{C_2}{(1+y_1)^{T_2-1}} - \frac{1}{(1+y_1)^{T_2}}$$

The zero-coupon yield at maturity T2 can then be estimated by solving the following equation for y2:

$$R_2 = \frac{1}{(1+y_2)^{T_2}}$$

This process is repeated for all the remaining bonds, resulting in a set of n zero-coupon yields that are consistent with the observed bond prices. These yields can then be used to construct the zero-coupon yield curve, which is a function that maps bond maturities to zero-coupon yields.

Overall, the bootstrapping technique is a powerful tool for yield curve construction, as it provides a way to estimate the zero-coupon yield curve using only a set of observable bond prices. However, the technique relies on a number of assumptions about the underlying bond market, such as the absence of arbitrage opportunities and the existence of a unique zero-coupon yield curve, and it requires careful consideration of a number of practical issues, such as the choice of interpolation method and the treatment of missing data.

Chapter 4

Advanced

4.1 Can you explain the concept of cointegration and its application in pairs trading strategies?

Cointegration is the statistical relationship between two or more time series, indicating that they move together over time despite short-term divergences. In other words, cointegration measures the long-term relationship between two or more variables.

Cointegration is particularly relevant to pairs trading strategies, which aim to profit from the divergence of two closely related assets. In pairs trading, two assets that have a long-term relationship are identified and traded based on the expectation that a short-term deviation from their long-term relationship will eventually revert to the mean.

To identify potential pairs for trading, pairs traders often use statistical measures such as the correlation coefficient between the two assets, but correlation only measures how two series move together in the short term, not the long term. Cointegration, on the other hand, provides a more reliable measure of the long-term relationship between two assets because it accounts for the fact that their prices may not move in perfect lockstep.

Once a cointegrated pair has been identified, pairs traders typically take a mean-reverting approach to trading. The basic idea of mean reversion is that if the prices of two assets have diverged significantly from their long-term mean, they are likely to revert to that mean eventually, providing an opportunity to profit from the expected convergence.

For example, suppose a pairs trader identifies a cointegrated pair of stocks, A and B, and observes that the ratio of their prices is currently significantly above its long-term mean. The trader might buy stock A and short sell an equivalent value of stock B, betting that the ratio will eventually revert to its mean and that the profits from the short sale will more than offset any losses on the long position. If the trader's analysis was correct, they will make a profit as the prices eventually converge.

In summary, cointegration is a powerful tool for identifying pairs for trading and assessing the long-term relationship between two assets. Pairs traders can leverage this relationship to develop mean-reverting strategies that aim to profit from short-term divergences between the two assets.

4.2 How do you use Principal Component Analysis (PCA) in quantitative finance, and what insights can it provide?

Principal Component Analysis (PCA) is a widely used statistical technique in quantitative finance for dimensionality reduction and risk management. It is a mathematical tool that can be used to identify the underlying structure in data and to transform data into a form that is easier to work with.

PCA is used in finance to analyze large datasets and to identify hidden patterns that may not be immediately apparent. By reducing the number of variables in a dataset, PCA can help to simplify complex financial models, making them easier to compute and understand.

One of the main applications of PCA in finance is in risk management. By identifying the principal components in a portfolio of financial assets, investors can estimate the risk of the portfolio and make informed decisions about how to allocate their assets. PCA can also be used to construct portfolios that are optimized for risk and return.

Another important application of PCA in finance is in the analysis of financial markets. By applying PCA to a large dataset of stock prices, for example, investors can identify hidden patterns in the data that may be indicative of future market movements. This can help investors to make more informed investment decisions and to mitigate risk.

In general, PCA can provide insights into the underlying structure of complex financial datasets. By identifying the principal components of a dataset, investors can gain a better understanding of the relationships between different variables and can use this knowledge to develop more accurate financial models.

To illustrate how PCA can be used in finance, consider an example in which an investor wants to analyze the returns of a portfolio of stocks over a period of time. The investor has data on the daily returns of 20 stocks over a one-year period. The dataset has 252 rows (one for each trading day) and 20 columns (one for each stock).

To apply PCA to this dataset, the investor first calculates the covariance matrix of the dataset. The covariance matrix is a measure of the degree to which each stock's returns are related to the other stocks' returns. Using the covariance matrix, the investor then identifies the principal components of the dataset. These principal components are linear combinations of the original variables (in this case, the stock returns) that capture most of the variance in the dataset.

The investor can then use the principal components to calculate the risk of the portfolio. By choosing the appropriate number of principal components, the investor can obtain an estimate of the risk of the portfolio that is more accurate than using all 20 stocks individually. This can be particularly useful in cases where the number of variables is large and complex, and it is difficult to obtain accurate estimates of the risk of the portfolio.

Overall, PCA is a powerful tool that can be used to analyze complex financial datasets and to gain insights into the underlying structure of financial markets. By identifying the principal components of a dataset, investors can develop more accurate financial models, manage risk more effectively, and make more informed investment decisions.

4.3 What is the role of stochastic processes in quantitative finance, and can you provide an example?

Stochastic processes play a fundamental role in quantitative finance because financial markets are inherently uncertain and unpredictable. Stochastic processes are mathematical models that capture the randomness and uncertainty of market phenomena, such as asset prices, interest rates, and volatility. These models are essential for pricing financial instruments, assessing risk, and designing investment strategies.

One of the most widely used stochastic processes in quantitative finance is the geometric Brownian motion (GBM) process. GBM is used to model the evolution of asset prices, such as stocks, currencies, and commodities. The GBM process assumes that the asset price follows a log-normal distribution, which reflects the tendency of prices to exhibit fat tails and skewness. The GBM process is described by the following stochastic differential equation:

$$dS_t = \mu S_t dt + \sigma S_t dW_t$$

where S_t is the asset price at time t, μ is the drift or expected return, σ is the volatility or standard deviation, W_t is a Brownian motion or Wiener process. The term dW_t represents the infinitesimal change in W_t over an infinitesimal time interval dt. The GBM process can be simulated using Monte Carlo

methods, which involve randomly drawing samples from the
log-normal distribution and simulating the evolution of the asset price over time.

An example of the application of stochastic processes in quantitative finance is the pricing of options using the Black-Scholes
model. The Black-Scholes model is based on the assumption
that the underlying asset follows a GBM process, and it provides a closed-form solution for the price of a European call
option. The Black-Scholes formula is given by:

$$C(S_t, K, r, \sigma, T) = S_t N(d_1) - K e^{-rT} N(d_2)$$

where C is the price of the call option, S_t is the current price
of the underlying asset, K is the strike price, r is the risk-free
interest rate, σ is the volatility, T is the time to maturity, $N()$
is the cumulative standard normal distribution, and d_1 and d_2
are defined as:

$$d_1 = \frac{\ln(S_t/K) + (r + \sigma^2/2)T}{\sigma\sqrt{T}}, \quad d_2 = d_1 - \sigma\sqrt{T}$$

The Black-Scholes formula shows that the price of a call option
depends on the current price of the underlying asset, the strike
price, the interest rate, the volatility, and the time to maturity.
The formula also reflects the probabilistic nature of option pricing, as it involves the cumulative standard normal distribution,
which is a function of probability. Therefore, the Black-Scholes
model illustrates the importance of stochastic processes in modeling and pricing financial instruments.

4.4 How do you apply machine learning techniques to financial data analysis and prediction?

Machine learning techniques are increasingly being applied in financial data analysis and prediction due to the massive amount of data available in the financial industry. These techniques utilize algorithms that can learn from historical data to make predictions or decisions without being explicitly programmed.

One common application of machine learning in finance is the prediction of stock prices or market trends. This involves training a machine learning algorithm on historical data of stock prices, trading volumes, company financial statements, news sentiment, etc. The algorithm then uses the learned patterns to make predictions about future prices, which can be used by investors to make trading decisions.

Another application of machine learning in finance is in credit risk analysis. Banks and lenders use historical data on borrowers to train machine learning models to predict the likelihood of default or delinquency. The models can consider factors such as credit score, income, employment history, and debt-to-income ratio to make predictions.

Machine learning techniques can also be used for fraud detection and prevention in the financial industry. By analyzing large volumes of transactions and customer behavior, machine learning models can identify patterns that indicate fraudulent activity and alert relevant parties for further investigation.

One popular machine learning technique for finance data analysis and prediction is the use of neural networks. Neural networks can model complex non-linear relationships between different variables, making them well-suited for financial data analysis where there are often many interconnected factors influencing outcomes. Other commonly used techniques include decision trees, random forests, support vector machines, and regression models.

In conclusion, machine learning techniques are increasingly being employed in the financial industry due to the large amount of data available, and their ability to analyze and extract value from such data. By training algorithms on historical data, these techniques are able to make predictions and provide insights that can help investors and financial institutions make better decisions.

4.5   What are the main types of algorithmic trading strategies, and how do they work?

Algorithmic trading refers to the use of computer programs to execute trades in financial markets, based on pre-determined rules and algorithms. The goal of algorithmic trading is typically to take advantage of market inefficiencies, generate profits, and/or reduce transaction costs. There are a wide range of algorithmic trading strategies, but some of the main types are described below:

1. Trend-following strategies: These strategies attempt to profit from market trends by analyzing past price data and identifying patterns that may indicate the direction of future price movements. One approach is to use moving averages to identify the

overall trend of the market, and to enter long or short positions accordingly. Another approach is to use technical indicators such as Relative Strength Index (RSI) or Moving Average Convergence Divergence (MACD) to identify market momentum.

2. Mean-reversion strategies: These strategies aim to profit from temporary deviations in price from their underlying values. This can be achieved by buying when the price is below its average value and selling when it is above. Mean-reversion strategies can be profitable in more stable markets where prices tend to oscillate around a particular value, but may perform poorly in markets with persistent trend movements.

3. Arbitrage strategies: These strategies aim to exploit price differences between different markets or financial instruments. For example, a trader could buy an undervalued stock in one market and then sell it in another market where it is overvalued, locking in a profit from the price difference. Statistical arbitrage strategies attempt to exploit mispricing in correlated securities by simultaneously buying and selling multiple securities and taking advantage of the price oscillations.

4. News-based strategies: These strategies are based on news and information that affects the price of securities. For example, traders may use natural language processing algorithms to scan news articles and social media posts, and make trades based on the sentiment of the content. News-based strategies can be especially useful for short-term trading, but they require a sophisticated understanding of natural language processing and sentiment analysis techniques.

5. High-frequency trading strategies: HFT refers to a type of algorithmic trading that relies on powerful computers and fast data transmission technologies to execute trades at extremely

high speeds. HFT strategies often involve large numbers of small trades executed at very high frequency to take advantage of small price differences or volatility. These strategies require large investments in technology and infrastructure, and are usually used by institutional investors.

In summary, algorithmic trading relies on the use of computer programs to make trading decisions based on pre-determined rules and algorithms. There are a wide range of algorithmic trading strategies, each with their own advantages and challenges. Successful algorithmic trading requires a combination of quantitative knowledge, technical expertise, and a deep understanding of market dynamics.

4.6   How do you manage model risk in quantitative finance?

Model risk refers to the risk of financial loss that arises from using flawed or inappropriate models to make important decisions. In quantitative finance, model risk can manifest itself in different ways, such as mispricing of financial instruments, inappropriate risk management, and incorrect evaluation of investment opportunities. As a result, it is essential to manage model risk effectively.

One of the key aspects of managing model risk is to ensure that the models used are appropriate for the task at hand. This involves carefully assessing the assumptions, limitations and performance of the model, as well as validating it using historical data and sensitivity analysis. The validation process should involve testing the model's accuracy and reliability under different scenarios and market conditions.

Another important strategy for managing model risk is to use multiple models for the same task and compare their results. This helps to identify any discrepancies between the models and to assess the uncertainty of the output. For example, in risk management, it is common to use two or more models to estimate the same risk metric and to compare the results to identify any inconsistencies.

The use of stress testing is also an effective tool for managing model risk. Stress testing involves subjecting the model to extreme scenarios and assessing the impact of these scenarios on the model's outputs. This helps to identify the limits of the model's validity and to quantify the potential losses that may result from extreme events.

Regular review and update of the model is also crucial in managing model risk. As market conditions change, models that were once valid may become unreliable or irrelevant. Thus, it is important to periodically review and update the assumptions, parameters and data used in the model. The review should involve input from a range of stakeholders including quants, traders, external auditors, and risk management professionals.

Finally, documentation is also an important aspect of managing model risk. Thorough documentation of the model development process, assumptions, inputs, testing, and validation is crucial in enabling other stakeholders to understand and critique the model. The documentation should also provide instructions on how to use the model, what it is expected to do, and what its limitations are.

Overall, model risk management is a process that involves careful assessment, validation, stress testing, and review of models. By implementing robust model risk management practices, quants and other stakeholders can ensure that models are reliable, relevant and provide accurate results.

4.7   Can you explain the concept of the Greeks in options pricing and risk management?

In options pricing and risk management, the Greeks are a set of parameters used to calculate the sensitivity of an option's price to changes in various factors such as the underlying asset's price, time to expiration, volatility, and interest rates. The Greeks play a significant role in options trading as they help traders and investors to evaluate the risks and potential profits associated with different options strategies.

Here are the most common Greeks used in options trading:

1. Delta: Delta measures the rate of change in an option's price relative to the underlying asset's price. It ranges from -1 to 1, with call options having a positive delta and put options having a negative delta. For example, if a call option has a delta of 0.5, it means that for every $1 increase in the underlying asset's price, the call option's price will increase by $0.5.

2. Gamma: Gamma measures the rate of change in an option's delta relative to changes in the underlying asset's price. It reflects the curvature of the option's price graph. Gamma is highest for at-the-money options and decreases as the option moves further in or out of the money.

3. Vega: Vega measures the rate of change in an option's price relative to changes in implied volatility. It is highest for at-the-money options and decreases as the option moves further in or out of the money. A high Vega indicates that changes in volatility will have a significant impact on the option's price, while a low Vega indicates that changes in volatility will have little effect.

4. Theta: Theta measures the rate of change in an option's price relative to changes in time to expiration. It represents the time decay of an option, specifically how much value it loses each day due to the passage of time. Theta is highest for at-the-money options and decreases as the option moves further in or out of the money.

5. Rho: Rho measures the rate of change in an option's price relative to changes in interest rates. It is highest for options with a long time to expiration and decreases as the option approaches expiration.

By monitoring the Greeks, traders can adjust their options positions to manage risk and maximize profits. For example, if a trader wants to hedge against price movements in the underlying asset, they can use delta-neutral strategies, where an equal number of options and shares are bought or sold. Similarly, if a trader expects volatility to increase, they can buy option contracts with a higher Vega.

4.8   How do you use Fourier transforms in quantitative finance, and what are their applications?

Fourier transform is a mathematical technique used to express a function as a sum of harmonic functions. In quantitative finance, Fourier transform had been widely used in option pricing, risk management, volatility estimation and extraction, and signal processing.

One of the most popular applications of Fourier transform in quantitative finance is in option pricing. The core of option pricing is evaluating expected discounted payoffs of the option under different underlying asset prices. Fourier transform can simplify the computation of these expected payoffs by transforming the option pricing equation from the time domain to the frequency domain. This approach is called the Fourier transform method for option pricing.

The basic idea behind the Fourier transform method is to first transform the option pricing equation from the time domain to the frequency domain. Then use the fast Fourier transform algorithm (FFT) to numerically evaluate the transformed equation. Finally, transform the results back to the time domain.

Another application of Fourier transform in quantitative finance is in volatility estimation and extraction. Volatility is a key factor that determines the pricing of many financial instruments. However, volatility is not directly observable, and often needs to be estimated or extracted from data. Fourier transform provides a powerful tool to estimate and extract volatility from financial time series.

One popular method is the Fourier-based estimator proposed by Andersen and Bollerslev (1998). The basic idea is to decompose the financial time series into different frequency components using Fourier transform. Then, estimate the volatility for each frequency component separately. This approach can capture the frequency-dependent property of volatility and improve the accuracy of volatility estimation.

To summarize, Fourier transform is a versatile tool in quantitative finance that can be used for option pricing, risk management, volatility estimation, and signal processing. Its applications are not limited to the ones mentioned above and are continually evolving.

4.9 What are the main differences between mean-variance optimization and mean-CVaR optimization in portfolio management?

Mean-variance optimization (MVO) is a widely used approach in portfolio management. It is a mathematical technique that aims to find the portfolio with the highest expected return for a given level of risk (measured as the portfolio variance).

On the other hand, mean-CVaR optimization (MCO) is a more recently developed approach that addresses some of the limitations of MVO. CVaR stands for Conditional Value at Risk, which is a risk measure that captures both the magnitude and the likelihood of extreme losses.

The main differences between MVO and MCO are:

1. Risk measure: MVO uses variance as a measure of risk, while MCO uses CVaR. CVaR is a more robust risk measure because it takes into account extreme events that can have a significant impact on the portfolio's performance.

2. Treatment of downside risk: MVO treats downside risk symmetrically with upside risk, while MCO places more emphasis on the downside. This means that MCO portfolios are typically more conservative and have a higher allocation to safe assets.

3. Solution approach: MVO is a quadratic programming problem that can be solved analytically. MCO is a nonlinear optimization problem that is more challenging to solve, but numerical methods are available.

4. Sensitivity to input parameters: MVO is highly sensitive to the input parameters, especially the expected returns and covariance matrix. In contrast, MCO is less sensitive to these parameters and can handle more complex and uncertain scenarios.

In summary, MCO is a more advanced method that can lead to better risk-adjusted returns, especially in turbulent markets where downside risk is a concern. However, MCO requires more sophisticated modeling and computation, and may be subject to estimation errors and parameter uncertainty.

4.10 What is the role of behavioral finance in understanding market inefficiencies, and how does it differ from traditional finance?

Behavioral finance is a subfield of finance that aims to explain why people make irrational decisions when it comes to financial matters. It seeks to understand how emotions, biases, and cognitive errors affect investor behavior and, consequently, financial markets. The role of behavioral finance in understanding market inefficiencies is significant because it suggests that market participants are not always rational in their decision-making, and as such, there are inefficiencies present in the market that can be exploited.

There are different ways in which behavioral finance differs from traditional finance. One of the main differences is that traditional finance assumes that market participants are rational and will always act in their best interests, whereas behavioral finance recognizes that investors are often influenced by emotions, biases, and other non-rational factors.

For example, when faced with uncertainty or ambiguity, investors may place too much weight on recent information or may rely too heavily on heuristics or rules of thumb. This can result in overreaction or underreaction to news, leading to market anomalies such as momentum or reversal effects.

Another way in which traditional finance and behavioral finance differ is in their approach to risk. Traditional finance assumes that investors are risk-averse and that they weigh the potential gains and losses of an investment equally. Behavioral finance, on the other hand, recognizes that investors may be risk-seeking, risk-averse, or exhibit different risk attitudes depending on the situation. Behavioral finance also acknowledges that investors may be more sensitive to losses than gains, which can lead to loss aversion.

Overall, the role of behavioral finance in understanding market inefficiencies is to identify and explain the anomalies or deviations from the efficient market hypothesis that cannot be fully explained by traditional finance. By taking into account the biases and emotions that affect investor behavior, behavioral finance offers a more nuanced understanding of financial markets and can help investors and practitioners make better decisions.

4.11   Can you explain the concept of regime-switching models and their application in finance?

Regime-switching models are a class of statistical models that allow the underlying parameters or properties of the model to change depending on the state of the economy. In finance, regime-switching models are widely used to capture the time-varying nature of financial markets and to model the behavior of financial assets under different economic conditions.

One common regime-switching model used in finance is the Hidden Markov Model (HMM). HMM is a statistical model that assumes the observed data is generated by a hidden (unobservable) Markov process. The HMM has two components: the Hidden Markov process and the observed data process. The Hidden Markov process is the one that switches between differ-

ent regimes, which are characterized by different distributions
of the observed data process.

For example, in stock price modeling, a regime-switching model
would assume that stock prices move differently in different economic conditions. For instance, if the economy is in a recession,
stock prices may exhibit greater volatility and exhibit negative
trends. Conversely, if the economy is in a boom, stock prices
may exhibit greater positive trends and be less volatile. A simple two-regime HMM model could therefore be set up as follows:

The Hidden Markov process could take two states: "Recession"
and "Boom", with recession and boom having different mean
and volatility parameters, and switching between the two states
governed by a Markov chain with transition probabilities between states.

The observed data process could be modeled with a normal
distribution for each regime, with different mean and covariance
parameters for each conditional distribution.

The parameters of the HMM can be estimated using Bayesian
methods or maximum likelihood estimation, and once fitted,
the model can be used for forecasting, portfolio optimization,
and risk management.

There are many other types of regime-switching models used
in finance, such as threshold autoregressive models, switching regression models, and regime-switching ARIMA. Each of
these models assumes different characteristics of the change in
regimes, and can be used in different applications in finance,
such as predicting asset prices, modeling interest rates, or managing portfolio risk. Regime-switching models are effective because they allow for more accurate and robust financial model-

ing in real-world situations, where financial markets can exhibit abrupt changes in behavior based on economic conditions.

4.12   What is the role of jump diffusion models in the pricing of financial derivatives?

Jump diffusion models are used in the pricing of financial derivatives to account for events that cause asset value jumps (discontinuities) within an underlying asset price process. A jump diffusion model combines a Brownian motion process with a compound Poisson process that represents the jump component.

The Brownian motion component represents diffusion or regular price changes, while the Poisson component represents infrequent jumps. These jumps may be caused by events such as news releases, economic data announcements, or exogenous shocks to the market.

Jump diffusion models provide a better framework to capture extreme price movements, which are not well-captured by a purely continuous diffusion model. They are particularly useful in modeling prices of assets with kurtosis higher than that of the normal distribution, such as equity prices, commodity prices, and foreign exchange rates.

The presence of jumps creates additional risk, and hence, affects the value of options and other derivatives. Pricing of jump models can be done using Monte Carlo simulation or using Fourier transform methods.

One commonly used jump diffusion model is the Merton model, which assumes that the underlying asset price process follows a log-normal distribution, modified by a compound Poisson process. The compound Poisson process represents the jump component, and the model is parameterized by the intensity of the jump process and the volatility of the asset price. Other popular jump diffusion models include the Bates model and Kou model, which allow for stochastic volatility in addition to jumps in the asset price.

In summary, jump diffusion models play a crucial role in financial derivative pricing by providing a more accurate description of asset price movements and allowing for the inclusion of infrequent but disruptive jumps in the underlying asset price process.

4.13 How do you measure tail risk in a portfolio, and what strategies can be used to mitigate it?

Tail risk refers to the likelihood of extreme negative events that occur beyond what is normally expected or predicted by a probability distribution. In a financial context, tail risk is the probability of experiencing losses that are much larger than what would be expected based on historical data or statistical models. Managing and mitigating tail risk in a portfolio is an essential part of risk management.

There are several ways to measure tail risk in a portfolio. One of the most popular methods is Value at Risk (VaR), which measures the potential loss that a portfolio could suffer over a specified holding period at a given confidence level. VaR estimates the maximum potential loss a portfolio could suffer over a specified holding period at a certain probability level. However, VaR measures can underestimate tail risk since it assumes that the probability distribution of returns is normal, which may not be the case in real-world situations.

Another measure of tail risk is Conditional Value at Risk (CVaR), also known as Expected Shortfall. CVaR measures the average loss of the tail of the distribution beyond the VaR threshold. It provides an estimate of the expected loss that will be incurred in the worst-case scenario beyond the VaR level. CVaR can be a more useful measure of tail risk because it accounts for extreme losses that VaR does not consider.

Tail risk can be mitigated by incorporating diversification and hedging techniques. Diversification across different asset classes that have low correlation with each other can reduce portfolio risk. Adding uncorrelated assets to a portfolio can reduce the risk of a tail event affecting the entire portfolio. Hedging techniques like portfolio insurance or using options can also reduce tail risk. Strategies like put options can be implemented to protect against negative tail risk events that could decimate a portfolio.

Another strategy to mitigate tail risk is tail risk parity. In tail risk parity, the portfolio is constructed so that each asset contributes equally to the tail risk of the portfolio. This strategy is based on the idea that not all risk is created equal, and some assets are more exposed to tail risk than others. By balancing the tail risk across the portfolio, tail risk parity aims to create a more robust portfolio that can withstand extreme events.

In conclusion, tail risk is an important factor to consider when managing a portfolio. Measuring tail risk can give valuable insight into the potential losses a portfolio could suffer beyond what is considered normal. Strategies like diversification, hedging, and tail risk parity can help mitigate tail risk and create a more resilient portfolio.

4.14 What are the main types of fixed income strategies, and how do they work?

There are several different types of fixed income strategies that investors can use to achieve various investment goals. Here are some of the main fixed income strategies:

1. Buy and Hold: This is a simple fixed income strategy where an investor buys a bond and holds it until it matures. The investor receives coupon payments during the life of the bond and gets their principal back at maturity. The returns for this strategy are fixed and known at the time of purchase.

2. Yield Curve Strategies: These strategies aim to take advantage of changes in the shape of the yield curve. A yield curve is a graph that plots interest rates versus the time to maturity for a range of fixed income securities. By analyzing the yield curve, investors can choose different maturities of bonds to buy and sell in order to profit from changes in the shape of the curve. For example, if the yield curve is steepening (short-term rates are falling faster than long-term rates), an investor could buy long-term bonds and sell short-term bonds to profit from the higher yield differential.

3. Credit Strategies: These strategies involve investing in bonds with different credit ratings. Bonds with higher credit ratings (like AAA or AA) typically have lower yields, while bonds with lower credit ratings (like BB or B) have higher yields but are also riskier. By choosing bonds with different credit ratings, investors can potentially earn higher yields while managing the risk of defaults.

4. Duration Strategies: Duration is a measure of a bond's sensitivity to changes in interest rates. This strategy involves buying bonds with a certain duration and then hedging the interest rate risk by selling futures contracts or buying interest rate swaps. By managing the duration of the portfolio, investors can potentially lock in a certain yield and reduce the risk of interest rate fluctuations.

5. Convexity Strategies: Convexity is a measure of a bond's sensitivity to changes in interest rates and its curvature. This strategy involves buying bonds with high convexity (which means they have a more curved relationship between price and yield) and then hedging the interest rate risk with options. This strategy can potentially earn higher returns while also reducing the risk of interest rate fluctuations.

6. Mortgage-Backed Securities (MBS) Strategies: MBS are fixed income securities that are backed by a pool of mortgage loans. These strategies involve investing in MBS and hedging the risks with interest rate swaps or options. By analyzing the underlying mortgage pool, investors can potentially earn higher returns than traditional bonds while also managing the risk of prepayments.

Overall, fixed income strategies can be used to achieve various investment goals, from generating steady income to managing risk and volatility. It is important to carefully analyze the risks and potential returns of each strategy before investing.

4.15 Can you explain the concept of market microstructure and its relevance to high-frequency trading?

Market microstructure refers to the process by which financial transactions are executed and how prices are determined in a market. It encompasses the rules, mechanisms, and institutions that govern the trading process, such as exchange rules, order types, market participants, and trading strategies. Market microstructure plays an important role in determining the liquidity, efficiency, and fairness of a market, and it's crucial for understanding how financial markets function.

High-frequency trading (HFT) is a trading strategy that uses advanced algorithms and high-speed trading platforms to execute trades rapidly and exploit small price movements in financial markets. HFT relies heavily on market microstructure, as the speed and efficiency of trade execution can have a significant impact on HFT profitability. In fact, HFT firms invest heavily in technology and infrastructure to achieve the fastest possible trade execution and take advantage of market microstructure inefficiencies.

One important aspect of market microstructure relevant to HFT is order flow. Order flow refers to the continuous stream of buy and sell orders that enter the market, and it can provide valuable information about market conditions and price movements. HFT firms closely monitor order flow and use it to make informed trading decisions, such as predicting future price movements based on the direction and size of orders.

Another important aspect of market microstructure is the impact of trades on market prices. When a large trade is executed, it can move the market price and create temporary imbalances in supply and demand. HFT firms use sophisticated algorithms to time their trades and minimize the impact of their orders on market prices, as even small price movements can erode their profitability.

Overall, understanding market microstructure is essential for successful HFT strategies. HFT firms employ a range of tactics and techniques to exploit market microstructure inefficiencies, and the speed and efficiency of trade execution can have a significant impact on HFT profitability.

4.16   How do you use copulas in the modeling of joint default probabilities?

Copulas are statistical tools that are widely used in the modeling of joint probabilities of several risk variables. They allow us to model the dependence between different variables separately from their marginal distributions. This way, we are able to capture the complex interdependence between variables that would be difficult to model otherwise.

In the context of default-risk modeling, copulas can be used to model the dependence between the default events of several firms or assets. The joint probability of multiple defaults can be challenging to estimate since it involves modeling the dependence structure between the default events of individual firms, while also considering the marginal probabilities of default of each individual firm. Copula modeling addresses these challenges by modeling the dependence structure of the defaults directly, without relying on the individual marginal probabilities solely.

The first step in constructing a copula-based model of joint default probabilities is to choose a suitable copula function. There are several families of copulas to choose from, each with different properties that can be exploited depending on the specific context. In practice, common choices include Archimedean copulas, elliptical copulas, and vine copulas.

Once a copula function has been chosen, it can be parameterized to fit the specific dependence structure of the variables being modeled. This is usually done by fitting the copula to observed data on the joint default events of several firms.

Finally, the copula-based model can be used to estimate probabilities of multiple defaults by generating random samples from the fitted copula and mapping them to the individual default probabilities of each firm. This way, we can simulate multiple realizations of the joint default events of several firms, which can be used to generate estimates of risk metrics such as the Expected Loss or Economic Capital.

In summary, copulas provide a powerful tool for modeling the dependence between multiple default events of individual firms or assets. By allowing for separate modeling of the dependence structure and the marginal probabilities, copulas can lead to more accurate modeling of joint default probabilities and estimates of risk metrics.

Below is an example of how to fit a Gaussian copula and estimate joint default probabilities using Python:

```
import pandas as pd
import numpy as np
import scipy.stats as stats

# Load data on individual default probabilities
defaults = pd.read_csv('default_probs.csv')

# Fit Gaussian copula to logit-transformed defaults
logit_defaults = stats.norm.ppf(defaults)
G = np.corrcoef(logit_defaults.T)
n = len(defaults)
gc = stats.multivariate_normal(cov=G)
u = gc.rvs(size=10000)

# Generate samples of joint defaults and map to individual defaults
sim_defaults = pd.DataFrame(stats.norm.cdf(u), columns=defaults.
    columns)
sim_defaults['joint_default'] = sim_defaults.prod(axis=1)

# Estimate joint default probabilities and report Expected Loss
joint_probs = sim_defaults['joint_default'].mean()
exp_loss = joint_probs * total_portfolio_exposure
```

4.17   What are the main challenges in modeling and forecasting financial time series?

Modeling and forecasting financial time series are important endeavors in quantitative finance, as they involve developing statistical methods to predict future prices, returns, and volatilities of financial assets such as stocks, bonds, commodities, and currencies. However, financial time series data is characterized by several challenges that complicate the modeling and forecasting process. In this answer, we will discuss the main challenges in modeling and forecasting financial time series along with potential solutions and examples.

1. Non-stationarity

The first challenge in modeling financial time series is non-stationarity, which means that the statistical properties of the data change over time. This can include changes in volatility, trends, seasonality, and correlation structure. Non-stationarity can make it difficult to estimate model parameters and make accurate forecasts, as historical data may not be representative of future behavior.

Potential solutions to non-stationarity include using time series transformations such as differencing or detrending, using models that explicitly account for time-varying behavior, such as state-space models or regime-switching models, or using more advanced machine learning techniques such as deep learning or reinforcement learning.

Example: The volatility of equity returns tends to exhibit clustering, which means that periods of high volatility tend to be followed by periods of high volatility and vice versa. A common approach to modeling this behavior is to use a GARCH (generalized autoregressive conditional heteroskedasticity) model, which can capture time-varying volatility.

2. Non-linearity

The second challenge in modeling financial time series is non-linearity, which means that the relationship between variables is not a simple linear function. This can include non-linear trends, non-linear dependence, and non-linear feedback effects. Non-linearity can make it difficult to find a suitable functional form for the model and can lead to inaccurate forecasts.

Potential solutions to non-linearity include using non-linear regression models such as exponential smoothing, neural networks, or support vector machines, or using more advanced

machine learning techniques such as deep learning or reinforcement learning.

Example: The price of commodities such as oil or gold often exhibit non-linear patterns such as mean reversion or long-term
cycles. A common approach to modeling this behavior is to use
a nonlinear autoregressive model such as an ARIMA (autoregressive integrated moving average) model.

3. High-dimensional data

The third challenge in modeling financial time series is the high-
dimensional nature of financial data. This means that there are
often many variables (such as stock prices, interest rates, and
economic indicators) that can be used to predict the behavior of financial markets. However, high-dimensional data can
lead to overfitting and spurious results, which can lead to poor
forecasts.

Potential solutions to high-dimensional data include using dimension reduction techniques such as principal component analysis or factor analysis, using regularization techniques such as
Lasso or Ridge regression, or using more advanced machine
learning techniques such as random forests or gradient boosting
machines.

Example: The pricing of mortgage-backed securities (MBS)
is influenced by many economic and financial variables such
as interest rates, housing prices, and unemployment rates. A
common approach to modeling this behavior is to use a factor
model, which decomposes the data into a few underlying factors
that explain the majority of the variation.

In conclusion, modeling and forecasting financial time series is a challenging task due to the non-stationarity, non-linearity, and high-dimensional nature of financial data. However, there are many potential solutions to these challenges, including using time series transformations, non-linear models, dimension reduction techniques, and machine learning methods. It is critical to carefully select the appropriate methods for each unique financial time series and to regularly check and adjust the model parameters as new data becomes available.

4.18   How do you assess the performance of a trading strategy or investment model?

There are various ways to assess the performance of a trading strategy or investment model. Here are some widely used methods:

1. Sharpe Ratio: The Sharpe Ratio measures the excess return per unit of risk taken. It is calculated as:

$$Sharpe\ Ratio = \frac{R_p - R_f}{\sigma_p}$$

Where R_p is the average return of the strategy, R_f is the risk-free rate, and σ_p is the standard deviation of the strategy's returns. Generally, a Sharpe Ratio greater than 1 indicates good performance.

2. Maximum Drawdown: The maximum drawdown measures the largest loss from a peak to a trough of an investment portfolio. It is calculated as:

$$Maximum\ Drawdown = \frac{P_{peak} - P_{trough}}{P_{peak}}$$

Where P_{peak} and P_{trough} are the highest and lowest portfolio values, respectively. Generally, a smaller maximum drawdown indicates better performance.

3. Risk-Adjusted Return: The risk-adjusted return is a measure of the return per unit of risk taken. It is calculated as:

$$Risk - Adjusted\ Return = \frac{R_p - R_f}{\beta}$$

Where R_p is the average return of the strategy, R_f is the risk-free rate, and β is the beta of the strategy (i.e., its sensitivity to market movements). A higher risk-adjusted return indicates better performance.

4. Cumulative Return: The cumulative return is the total return earned over a period of time. It is calculated as:

$$Cumulative\ Return = \frac{P_t - P_0}{P_0}$$

Where P_t and P_0 are the portfolio values at the end and beginning of the period, respectively. A higher cumulative return indicates better performance.

5. Backtesting: Backtesting is the process of testing a strategy on historical data to see how it would have performed in the past. This can provide insight into the strategy's potential future performance. However, it is important to be cautious

when relying solely on backtesting results, as past performance does not guarantee future results.

Overall, assessing the performance of a trading strategy or investment model requires considering multiple factors related to returns, risk, and other metrics. It is important to use a combination of methods and to perform regular assessments over time to ensure that the strategy continues to perform as expected.

4.19 Can you explain the concept of dynamic asset allocation and its benefits in portfolio management?

Dynamic asset allocation (DAA) is an investment strategy that aims to adjust the composition of a portfolio over time in response to changing market conditions. This involves shifting the allocation of assets between different investment categories such as equities, fixed income, commodities, and cash according to a set of pre-determined rules or models that take into account various factors such as market volatility, economic indicators, and company fundamentals.

The primary benefit of dynamic asset allocation is its ability to help investors manage risk and enhance returns by adapting to changing market conditions. By allocating capital to those assets that are most likely to perform well in a particular environment, DAA strategies can help minimize downside risks while maximizing upside potential.

For instance, during times of market volatility or economic uncertainty, a DAA strategy might shift a larger portion of the portfolio into more stable, defensive assets such as bonds or cash, while reducing exposure to more volatile assets such as equities. This can help protect the portfolio from steep losses while still allowing investors to capture some upside potential.

Conversely, during times of strong market growth or positive economic indicators, a DAA strategy might increase exposure to equities and other high-growth assets to capitalize on potential returns. This can help enhance total portfolio returns while balancing risk exposure.

One of the challenges of implementing a DAA strategy is selecting the right models or rules to guide asset allocation decisions. Some DAA strategies rely on simple moving averages or technical indicators to make allocation decisions, while others use more sophisticated quantitative models that take into account a wide range of market and economic data. The effectiveness of a DAA strategy will ultimately depend on the quality of these models and the ability of the investor or fund manager to implement them consistently and effectively.

Overall, however, dynamic asset allocation can be a valuable tool for investors seeking to manage risk, enhance returns, and take advantage of changing market conditions.

4.20 What are the main regulatory requirements and ethical considerations in the field of quantitative finance?

The field of quantitative finance is subject to a number of regulatory requirements and ethical considerations. In general, quantitative finance involves the application of advanced mathematical and statistical techniques to the analysis of financial markets and the development of trading and investment strategies. As such, there are a number of laws and regulations that apply to the field, as well as ethical considerations that must be taken into account.

Regulatory Requirements: 1. Compliance with financial laws and regulations: The field of quantitative finance is subject to a range of financial laws and regulations, including securities laws, banking regulations, and tax laws. Financial institutions and individuals working in quantitative finance must comply with these laws and regulations, and failure to do so can result in legal penalties and other consequences.

2. Disclosure and reporting requirements: Financial institutions and individuals working in quantitative finance must also comply with disclosure and reporting requirements, such as the reporting of trading activity and the disclosure of conflicts of interest. Failure to comply with these requirements can result in legal and reputational consequences.

3. Risk management: Quantitative finance involves the management of financial risk, and financial institutions and individuals working in the field are subject to risk management requirements. These can include stress testing, scenario analysis, and other techniques designed to identify and manage risk.

Ethical Considerations: 1. Confidentiality: Financial institutions and individuals working in quantitative finance often have access to confidential financial and market data. As such, there are ethical considerations related to maintaining the confidentiality of this data and using it only for legitimate business purposes.

2. Conflicts of interest: Financial institutions and individuals working in quantitative finance may have conflicts of interest that must be disclosed and managed appropriately. This can include conflicts related to the sale of financial products, the allocation of trades, and other areas.

3. Fair dealing: Financial institutions and individuals working in quantitative finance are subject to ethical considerations related to fair dealing, including the fair treatment of clients and other market participants.

4. Responsible use of models: Quantitative finance often involves the use of complex mathematical models to analyze financial markets and develop trading and investment strategies. However, there are ethical considerations related to the responsible use of these models, including the transparency and robustness of the models, and the appropriate use of assumptions and inputs.

Overall, the field of quantitative finance is subject to a range of regulatory requirements and ethical considerations, which must be taken into account by financial institutions and individuals working in the field. Failure to comply with these requirements can result in legal and reputational consequences, and can undermine the integrity of financial markets more broadly.

Chapter 5

Expert

5.1 Can you discuss the main differences between single-factor and multi-factor models in asset pricing?

In asset pricing, single-factor and multi-factor models are used to estimate the expected return of an asset, based on its exposure to different types of risk factors. The main difference between the two models is the number of risk factors that are included in the analysis.

A single-factor model assumes that the asset's return is primarily driven by one factor, typically the market index, known as the "systematic risk" or "market risk". This factor explains most of the variation in the asset's returns, and any additional risks are assumed to be diversifiable, uncorrelated to the market, and therefore irrelevant to the asset's expected return. A

well-known example of a single-factor model is the Capital Asset Pricing Model (CAPM), which assumes that the expected
return of an asset is proportional to its beta (systematic risk)
times the market risk premium.

$$E(R_i) = R_f + \beta_i \cdot (E(R_M) - R_f)$$

where $E(R_i)$ is the expected return of asset i, R_f is the risk-free
rate, β_i is the asset's beta, $E(R_M)$ is the expected return of the
market, and $E(R_M) - R_f$ is the market risk premium.

A multi-factor model, on the other hand, incorporates multiple factors that may affect the asset's returns, beyond the
market risk factor. These factors could be industry-specific factors, such as interest rates, exchange rates, inflation, and other
macroeconomic variables. The multi-factor model provides a
more complex view of asset pricing, as it takes into account
how multiple factors may affect the expected returns of different assets.

Example of two-factor-model:

$$E(R_i) = R_f + \beta_{iM} \cdot (E(R_M) - R_f) + \beta_{iF} \cdot (E(R_F) - R_f)$$

where $E(R_i)$ is the expected return of asset i, R_f is the risk-free
rate, β_{iM} is the asset's beta to the market, β_{iF} is the asset's
beta to the second factor, and $E(R_M) - R_f$ and $E(R_F) - R_f$
are the market and second factor risk premiums, respectively.

The advantage of the multi-factor model is that it can capture
the impact of additional risk factors on an asset's return, which

may not be accounted for in the single-factor model. However, the more factors that are included in the analysis, the more complex the model becomes, and the more difficult it is to estimate the expected returns. Additionally, the presence of multiple factors can make it harder to interpret the significance of each factor, and can create collinearity problems that reduce the model's accuracy.

In summary, a single-factor model assumes that the asset's return is primarily driven by one factor, while a multi-factor model incorporates multiple factors. The choice between the two models depends on the complexity of the assets being priced, and the level of accuracy required for the analysis.

5.2 How do you incorporate transaction costs and market impact into your trading strategies?

Incorporating transaction costs and market impact is an essential aspect of any successful trading strategy in practice. In order to maximize profits, it is important to consider not only the expected return of a position, but also the costs associated with executing trades in the market. Here are some ways to incorporate transaction costs and market impact into trading strategies:

1. Cost-aware portfolio optimization: A cost-aware portfolio optimization technique is designed to incorporate transaction costs explicitly into the optimization problem. Traditional portfolio optimization techniques, such as the mean-variance optimization, aim to maximize the expected return under certain

risk constraints, but do not consider transaction costs. By contrast, a cost-aware portfolio optimization technique considers
both expected returns and transaction costs to minimize trading costs while achieving satisfactory portfolio performance.
One popular approach is to use quadratic programming with a
transaction cost constraint, such as the algorithm presented in
the paper "Optimal Trading with Alpha Predictors" by Robert
Almgren and Neil Chriss.

2. Smart order routing: Smart order routing is a technique
used by traders to minimize market impact costs and execution risk during trading. The aim is to find the best execution
venue and algorithm to execute a particular trade while minimizing the overall cost of trading. There are several smart order routing algorithms, such as volume-weighted average price
(VWAP), time-weighted average price (TWAP), and implementation shortfall. The goal is to minimize slippage, which is the
difference between the executed price of a trade and the market
price at the time of the order.

3. Quantify market impact costs: Market impact is the effect
of a particular order on the market, which can lead to changes
in prices and liquidity. It is an important cost to consider when
making trading decisions, as it can significantly impact the profitability of a trade. To account for market impact, traders must
quantify the expected costs of executing different trade sizes.
This can be done through empirical analysis of historical market data, or through the use of sophisticated models to estimate
market impact costs, such as the Almgren-Chriss model.

4. Algorithmic trading: Algorithmic trading involves using
computer algorithms to execute trades automatically. The aim
is to optimize the trade execution process by minimizing both
transaction costs and market impact. Algorithmic trading sys-

tems can use sophisticated algorithms, such as statistical arbitrage, trend-following, or mean-reversion, depending on the particular trading strategy. Algorithmic trading can also involve the use of artificial intelligence and machine learning techniques to optimize trading performance.

In summary, traders can incorporate transaction costs and market impact into trading strategies through techniques like cost-aware portfolio optimization, smart order routing, quantitative market impact analysis, and algorithmic trading. By taking into account these costs, traders can optimize their trading strategies to maximize profits and minimize overall costs.

5.3 Can you explain the concept of Bayesian statistics and how it can be applied in quantitative finance?

Bayesian statistics is a branch of statistics that allows for updating probabilities as new information becomes available. It is based on Bayes' theorem, which states that the probability of a hypothesis H given observed data D is proportional to the prior probability of H multiplied by the likelihood of D given H:

$$P(H|D) = \frac{P(D|H)P(H)}{P(D)}$$

where P(H|D) is the posterior probability of H given D, P(D|H) is the likelihood of D given H, P(H) is the prior probability of H, and P(D) is the probability of D.

In quantitative finance, Bayesian statistics can be applied to many different areas. One important application is in portfolio optimization, where it can be used to incorporate expert knowledge or prior beliefs into the investment process. For example, suppose an investor has a prior belief that a certain asset class is undervalued. Bayesian statistics can be used to update the investor's belief about the asset class as new information becomes available.

Another area where Bayesian statistics is commonly used is in the modeling of financial time series. A key challenge in modeling financial time series is dealing with the fact that the underlying processes may change over time. Bayesian statistics provides a framework for incorporating this uncertainty into the modeling process. For example, a Bayesian approach could be used to estimate the parameters of a time-varying volatility model such as GARCH (Generalized Autoregressive Conditional Heteroskedasticity). The Bayesian approach would provide a posterior distribution for the model parameters, which could be used to generate forecasts for future volatility.

Finally, Bayesian statistics can also be used in risk management. For example, Bayesian methods can be used to estimate the probability of extreme events such as market crashes or defaults. This information can then be used to inform risk management decisions such as what level of capital reserves should be held.

In summary, Bayesian statistics is a powerful tool that can be applied to many areas in quantitative finance. It allows for the incorporation of prior beliefs and expert knowledge, which can lead to more accurate estimates and better decision making.

5.4   What are the key differences between parametric and nonparametric estimation techniques, and when should each be used?

Parametric and nonparametric estimation techniques are two approaches used in estimating statistical models.

Parametric estimation is an approach that assumes a particular distributional form for the population, and the estimation process involves estimating the parameters of that distribution. Parametric models are typically more restrictive than nonparametric models, but they require fewer data points to estimate, and as a result, they often provide more accurate estimates when the underlying assumptions are satisfied. Examples of parametric models include linear regression, logistic regression, and normal distribution.

On the other hand, nonparametric estimation makes no assumptions about the underlying distribution of the population. Instead, the estimation process involves using the data to construct the estimator. Nonparametric models are often more flexible than parametric models, but they require more data points to estimate accurately. Examples of nonparametric models include kernel density estimation, spline regression, and decision trees.

In terms of when to use each approach, parametric models should be used when the underlying distributional assumptions are well understood and accurate, and when there is enough data to estimate the parameters of the model reliably. For example, if we know that the population follows a normal distribution and we have enough data, then a parametric model such as linear regression would be appropriate.

Nonparametric estimation should be used when there is not enough information about the population distribution, or when the underlying distribution assumptions are violated. Nonparametric models are also preferred when the data is of low dimensional or there is no exact probabilistic data descriptions. For example, kernel density estimation can be used to estimate the probability density function of a random variable, even when the underlying distribution is unknown and/or the sample size is small.

In summary, the choice between parametric and nonparametric estimation depends on the circumstances of the problem at hand. Understanding the strengths and limitations of each approach is important for selecting the most appropriate tool for a given project.

5.5   How do you manage the impact of data snooping bias in the development and evaluation of trading strategies?

Data snooping bias, also known as multiple hypothesis testing, occurs when a researcher repeatedly tests a hypothesis on the same dataset until a statistically significant result is found, without adjusting for the number of tests conducted. This can lead to finding false relationships and patterns in the data, which do not hold out-of-sample.

In quantitative finance, data snooping bias can be problematic in the development and evaluation of trading strategies, as it can lead to overfitting and incorrect assumptions about the predictive power of certain variables. To manage the impact of data snooping bias in the development and evaluation of trading strategies, several methods can be used:

1. Set aside a holdout sample: One approach to managing data snooping bias is to split the data into two subsets: one for developing the trading strategy and the other for evaluating its performance. This ensures that the performance of the trading strategy is evaluated on unseen data, preventing overfitting to the development sample.

2. Use out-of-sample testing: Another approach is to use out-of-sample testing, where the model is trained on one dataset and tested on another. This method ensures that the model's performance is evaluated on new and previously unseen data, reducing the risk of overfitting.

3. Adjust for multiple hypothesis testing: Researchers can also adjust for multiple hypothesis testing by using statistical methods such as the Bonferroni correction or False Discovery Rate (FDR) control. These methods adjust the p-value threshold for statistical significance based on the number of tests conducted, reducing the risk of false positives.

4. Cross-validation: Cross-validation is a technique used to estimate the performance of a model by training and testing it multiple times on different subsets of the data. This approach can help identify patterns and relationships that hold across different subsets of the data, and it can help avoid overfitting.

5. Be conservative in assumptions: Finally, researchers should be conservative in their assumptions about the predictive power

of variables and avoid using ad-hoc rules of thumbs for selecting variables or optimizing parameters. They should also be transparent about the methods used and document all steps taken in developing and evaluating the trading strategy.

In conclusion, to manage the impact of data snooping bias, quantitative analysts and researchers should use multiple methods and best practices like holdout samples, out-of-sample testing, statistical controls, cross-validation, and should be transparent about methods used.

5.6 What is the role of reinforcement learning in the development of algorithmic trading strategies?

Reinforcement learning (RL) is a type of machine learning in which an agent learns to make decisions based on trial and error interactions with an environment. RL has been applied in various domains, including finance, to develop automated trading strategies.

The role of reinforcement learning in the development of algorithmic trading strategies is to learn optimal trading decisions by maximizing a reward signal. In the context of trading, the reward signal could be defined in various ways, such as return on investment, Sharpe ratio, or profit and loss. The RL agent interacts with the market, observes the current state (e.g., asset prices, order books), takes an action (e.g., buy or sell), and receives a reward based on the outcome of the action. The agent's goal is to learn a policy that maximizes this cumulative reward over time.

One of the advantages of using RL in trading is that it can adapt to changing market conditions. As the market evolves, the optimal trading policy may change, and RL algorithms can learn to adapt to these changes. Additionally, RL algorithms can incorporate a wide range of information when making trading decisions, including technical indicators, market news, and trade volumes.

One common RL algorithm used in trading is Q-learning. Q-learning is a type of RL algorithm that learns the optimal action-value function Q^* in a tabular form. The action-value function estimates the expected cumulative reward of taking a particular action in a given state, following a certain policy. In trading, the policy could be defined as a function of various indicators, such as moving averages, or other market-based signals. The Q-learning algorithm learns this function iteratively by updating the Q-values based on the observed rewards, using the Bellman equation.

Another popular RL algorithm for trading is Deep Q-Networks (DQNs), which extends Q-learning to work with high-dimensional inputs such as images or time series data. DQNs use deep neural networks to approximate the Q-values; these networks can learn hidden representations of the input data that are relevant for making trading decisions. Reinforcement learning algorithms can also be combined with other machine learning techniques such as sentiment analysis, natural language processing, or clustering.

However, the use of RL in trading strategies does come with some caveats, including the risks of overfitting, underperformance, and difficulty in interpreting the resulting strategies. One should also consider legal and ethical implications of implementing fully automated trading systems.

To conclude, reinforcement learning has an important role in the development of algorithmic trading strategies by enabling the learning of optimal trading decisions based on market conditions. Q-learning and Deep Q-Networks are popular RL algorithms used in trading, and can be extended to incorporate a wide range of market data. While RL-based trading strategies can provide some benefits, they should be carefully evaluated before use in real-world scenarios.

5.7   How do you incorporate fat-tailed distributions into risk management and portfolio optimization models?

Incorporating fat-tailed distributions is essential for accurate risk management and portfolio optimization models as these distributions capture the likelihood of extreme events that may have significant impact on the portfolio. There are various approaches to incorporate fat-tailed distributions, each with its own advantages and disadvantages.

One approach is to use non-parametric methods such as historical simulation or bootstrapping, which are based on observed data rather than assuming a particular distribution. In these methods, a large number of scenarios are generated by resampling historical data or using Monte Carlo simulation, and portfolio returns are calculated for each scenario. The distribution of portfolio returns is then used to estimate risk measures and optimize the portfolio. While these methods are flexible and can capture complex distributional shapes, they require a large amount of data and may not be suitable for portfolios with limited historical data.

Another approach is to use parametric distributions with fat tails such as the Student's t-distribution, the Generalized Extreme Value distribution or the Generalized Pareto distribution. These distributions are commonly used in finance as they can capture the impact of extreme events. However, it is important to note that these distributions require estimation of parameters which may not always be straightforward and may require assumptions about the underlying distribution.

One specific example of how these distributions can be used is in Value-at-Risk (VaR) calculations. Traditional VaR methods assume a normal distribution of returns, which can underestimate the potential extreme losses. Incorporating a fat-tailed distribution allows for a more accurate estimate of the VaR by capturing the potential for tail events.

In portfolio optimization, incorporating fat-tailed distributions means that investors are taking into account the potential for large losses and tail events in their risk management plan. This may result in lower weights in assets with the potential for extreme losses and higher weights in assets that can act as hedges. Furthermore, incorporating fat-tailed distributions also allows for a more accurate estimation of portfolio returns and risk measures, which can lead to better portfolio optimization decisions.

Overall, incorporating fat-tailed distributions is an important component for accurate risk management and portfolio optimization models. The approach chosen should be based on the available data and the specific needs of the investor. It is important to consider both non-parametric and parametric methods, as each has its own advantages and disadvantages.

5.8   Can you discuss the key challenges and solutions for incorporating intraday data into quantitative models?

Incorporating high frequency (intraday) data into quantitative models offers great potential for improving our understanding of financial markets and making better investment decisions. However, it also presents some challenges that need to be addressed. In this response, I will discuss the main challenges and some solutions for incorporating intraday data into quantitative models.

Challenges:

1. **Data quality and consistency:** One of the biggest challenges of using intraday data is ensuring the quality and consistency of the data. Intraday data is often noisy and can contain errors, which can affect the accuracy of analyses and models.

2. **Data volume and storage:** Intraday data can be vast, and storing it can be costly. It is essential to have a robust data storage infrastructure that can handle large volumes of data.

3. **Computation time and complexity:** Intraday data models require complex computations that can be time and resource-intensive. This can make it challenging to build models within certain time constraints.

4. **Model robustness:** Models based on intraday data can be sensitive to changes in market conditions or inputs. This makes them less robust, and they may not perform as well in different market conditions.

Solutions:

1. **Data filtering and pre-processing:** To deal with the issue of data quality and consistency, it is important to apply filtering and pre-processing techniques before performing any analysis. This will help to remove noise and outliers in the data and ensure consistency.

2. **Data storage optimization:** To handle the challenges of data volume and storage, it may be necessary to optimize data storage by using compression techniques and storing only necessary data.

3. **Parallel processing:** To reduce the time and resource-intensive computations involved in building models based on intraday data, we can use parallel processing techniques that distribute the computation workload over multiple processors.

4. **Model diversification:** To improve model robustness, we need to diversify the models we use so that we have models suitable for different market conditions. We can also use ensemble techniques that combine multiple models to improve overall performance.

In summary, incorporating intraday data into quantitative models can bring significant benefits, but it also presents challenges that must be addressed. Good data quality and consistency, efficient data storage, parallel processing, and model diversification can help manage these challenges and enable the development of robust intraday models.

5.9   How do you account for structural breaks and regime shifts when modeling financial time series data?

Structural breaks and regime shifts are common in financial time series data, and can significantly affect the performance of statistical models. There are several approaches to account for these changes, including detecting the breaks and estimating the parameters separately for each regime, using regime-switching models, or using Bayesian methods with change-point priors.

One common approach to detecting structural breaks is to perform a Chow test. The Chow test is a statistical test that compares the variance of the estimated regression coefficients before and after a potential structural break. The test statistic is given by:

$$F = \frac{(RSS_R - RSS_{UR})/r}{RSS_{UR}/(n - k)}$$

where RSS_R is the residual sum of squares for the restricted model, $RSS_U R$ is the residual sum of squares for the unrestricted model, 'r' is the number of parameters in the restricted model, 'n' is the sample size, and 'k' is the number of parameters in the unrestricted model. If the test statistic is greater than a critical value, then we reject the null hypothesis that there is no structural break.

Another approach is to use regime-switching models, which explicitly model the changes in the data generating process. In a regime-switching model, the data is assumed to be generated by a finite number of regimes, each with its own set of parameters. The probability of being in each regime is modeled as a function of past observations. For example, a popular regime-switching model is the Markov-Switching Vector Autoregressive (MS-VAR) model. The MS-VAR model assumes that the data is generated by a finite number of regimes, each with its own VAR parameters. The probability of being in each regime is modeled as a function of past observations, and each regime is associated with a specific distribution of errors.

Another approach is to use Bayesian methods with change-point priors. In this approach, a prior is placed on the location of the structural break, and the posterior distribution is estimated via Markov Chain Monte Carlo (MCMC) simulation. For example, a popular prior for the location of the structural break is the Bayesian Lasso prior, which assumes that the coefficients before and after the break are sparse.

In conclusion, accounting for structural breaks and regime shifts is an important aspect of modeling financial time series data. Different approaches can be used such as detecting the breaks and estimating the parameters separately for each regime, using regime-switching models, or using Bayesian methods with change-point priors. The choice of the method should be motivated by the data and the research question at hand.

5.10 What are the main methods for incorporating market liquidity into portfolio optimization models?

Incorporating market liquidity into portfolio optimization models is a crucial aspect of portfolio management in order to take into account the impact of transaction costs on portfolio performance. Here are some of the methods that are commonly used to incorporate market liquidity into portfolio optimization models:

1. Bid-ask spread model: One way to estimate liquidity is to use the bid-ask spread as a proxy for transaction costs. This model assumes that transaction costs are proportional to the bid-ask spread of the security, which is the difference between the best available price at which a security can be sold and bought. The bid-ask spread can be estimated using historical data, such as the difference between the opening and closing prices or the highest and lowest prices of the day. The optimal portfolio can then be constructed using a utility function that incorporates this transaction cost measure.

2. Volume-impact model: Another approach is to use the volume of trading as a measure of liquidity. The volume-impact model assumes that as trade size increases, liquidity becomes more difficult to find and transaction costs increase. This method requires historical data on the relationship between trading volume and price impact, which can be used to estimate the cost of trading for different sizes of trade. An optimal portfolio can then be constructed using a utility function that incorporates this transaction cost measure.

3. Linear programming model: Linear programming models

can be used to optimize portfolios subject to transaction costs. These models typically use a quadratic cost function, where the cost of trading is a function of the difference between the current and desired portfolio weights, the transaction size, and the estimated transaction cost. The optimal portfolio is then determined by minimizing the total cost subject to a set of constraints, such as portfolio return or risk.

4. Dynamic programming model: Dynamic programming models can be used to optimize portfolios over a longer time horizon, taking into account the impact of transaction costs on future trading decisions. These models typically use a cost-to-go function that estimates the expected cost of trading over a given time period. The optimal trading strategy is then determined by minimizing the expected total cost of trading over the time horizon.

5. Monte Carlo simulation: Monte Carlo simulation can be used to estimate the impact of transaction costs on portfolio performance. This method involves generating random scenarios for asset returns and estimating the transaction costs associated with each scenario. The optimal portfolio can then be constructed by selecting the portfolio that provides the best trade-off between return and transaction costs across the different scenarios.

In all cases, it's important to note that incorporating market liquidity into portfolio optimization models is an approximation, and that actual transaction costs incurred may differ from those estimated by these models. It is important to use a combination of methods to obtain more accurate estimates of transaction costs, and to adjust investment decisions accordingly.

5.11 Can you explain the role of neural networks and deep learning in the analysis of financial data?

Neural networks and deep learning have emerged as powerful tools in the analysis of financial data due to their ability to analyze large amounts of complex data and identify underlying patterns and trends that may not be apparent using traditional statistical methods.

One of the key advantages of neural networks is their ability to learn from data without being explicitly programmed. Neural networks are comprised of interconnected neurons that are capable of processing and analyzing large amounts of data in parallel. The network is trained on a large dataset, and the weights of the neurons are adjusted until the network is able to accurately predict outcomes.

Deep learning goes one step further by using a more complex network architecture with multiple layers. This allows for the creation of more complex models that can identify more subtle patterns and trends in the data. Deep learning can be especially useful in financial analysis, as many financial datasets are characterized by high-dimensional data, non-linear relationships, and complex interactions between variables.

One example of the use of neural networks in financial analysis is in the prediction of stock prices. Traditional models for stock price prediction may be limited by their reliance on linear relationships between variables, while neural networks are able to capture more complex patterns and relationships that may be present in the data. For example, a popular approach for stock price prediction using neural networks is to use a recurrent neural network (RNN) to model the time series data for a particular stock. The RNN is able to capture the temporal dependencies within the data, allowing for more accurate predictions of future prices.

Another common application of neural networks in finance is in credit risk assessment. Banks and other financial institutions can use neural networks to analyze large amounts of data on borrowers and identify those with a high risk of default. For example, a neural network could be trained on past loan data to identify patterns that are associated with default risk, such as low credit scores or high debt-to-income ratios.

Overall, neural networks and deep learning have become increasingly important tools in the analysis of financial data due to their ability to analyze large amounts of complex data and identify underlying patterns and trends that would be difficult to detect using traditional statistical methods.

5.12   How do you incorporate sentiment analysis and alternative data sources into quantitative models?

Incorporating sentiment analysis and alternative data sources into quantitative models can add valuable insights to investment decisions. There are several approaches to incorporating these factors into models.

One approach is to treat sentiment analysis and alternative data as additional inputs to existing quantitative models. For example, a sentiment analysis score based on news headlines or social

media data can be included as an input into a stock price prediction model. Similarly, alternative data sources such as satellite
imagery showing changes in traffic or activity around potential investments can be incorporated as additional features into
models.

Another approach is to build entirely new models focused solely
on sentiment analysis or alternative data. These models may
use techniques such as machine learning to learn patterns and
relationships between the data and investment outcomes. For
example, a machine learning model may examine the relationship between social media sentiment and stock prices to generate predictions.

It is also essential to consider the quality and reliability of the
data sources used. A sentiment analysis score based on a small
sample size or biased data could lead to incorrect predictions.
Similarly, alternative data sources may have limitations or be
subject to errors in measurement. Therefore, a rigorous evaluation of data sources is essential before incorporating them into
models.

To illustrate this, let's consider an example of incorporating sentiment analysis into a stock price prediction model. Suppose we
have a dataset of historical stock prices and corresponding news
headlines. We can begin by calculating a sentiment score for
each headline using a natural language processing (NLP) technique such as the VADER algorithm. We can then include these
sentiment scores as an additional feature in a regression model
for predicting future stock prices. For instance, the model could
be:

$$Price_t = \beta_0 + \beta_1 * Price_{t-1} + \beta_2 * Sentiment_t + \epsilon_t$$

where $Price_t$ is the stock price at time t, $Sentiment_t$ is the sentiment score at time t, and β_1 and β_2 are coefficients to be estimated.

In conclusion, incorporating sentiment analysis and alternative data sources into quantitative models can provide valuable insights and improve investment decisions. However, it is crucial to carefully evaluate the data sources used and design models that appropriately capture the relationships between data and outcomes.

5.13 What are the main challenges in managing counterparty risk in the context of derivatives trading?

Counterparty risk is the risk that the other party to a financial contract may default on its obligations. In the context of derivatives trading, counterparty risk can be particularly pronounced due to the leverage and complexity inherent in these products. This makes managing counterparty risk a critical task for market participants, such as banks, hedge funds, and other financial institutions that engage in derivatives trading.

There are several main challenges involved in managing counterparty risk in the context of derivatives trading, which I will outline below:

1. Limited availability of data: Derivatives are often traded over-the-counter (OTC), which means they are not traded on a centralized exchange. As a result, the data on the market and the counterparties is often limited, which can make it difficult

to accurately assess counterparty risk.

2. Complexity of derivative products: Derivatives can be highly
complex financial instruments, making it difficult for market
participants to fully understand the risks they are taking on.
This complexity can also make it challenging to accurately value
these instruments, which can complicate efforts to manage counterparty risk.

3. Lack of standardization: There are a wide variety of derivative products, each with its own unique set of terms and conditions. This lack of standardization can make it difficult to
compare different products or to aggregate risk across different
counterparties.

4. Dynamic market conditions: Financial markets can be highly
volatile and can change rapidly. As a result, managing counterparty risk in the derivatives market requires ongoing monitoring
and analysis of market conditions and counterparties.

To address these challenges, market participants use a variety
of risk management techniques, which can include:

1. Collateralization: In derivatives trading, counterparties often exchange collateral to mitigate the risk of default. If one
counterparty defaults, the other party can use the collateral to
cover its losses.

2. Netting: Netting involves offsetting the amount owed to one
counterparty against the amount owed by the other counterparty. This can help to reduce the exposure to each counterparty.

3. Credit limits: Market participants may set limits on the
amount of risk they are willing to take on with a particular

counterparty. These limits can be based on factors such as creditworthiness, collateralization, and the counterparty's exposure to other positions.

4. VaR (Value-at-Risk) models: Market participants may use VaR models to estimate their potential losses from different types of risks, including counterparty risk. These models can help to identify potential problem areas and to quantify the potential impact of different scenarios.

Overall, managing counterparty risk in derivatives trading can be complex and challenging. Market participants need to carefully balance the potential rewards against the risks involved and use a range of risk management techniques to mitigate these risks.

5.14 How do you design and implement an effective stress-testing framework for a portfolio?

Designing and implementing an effective stress-testing framework involves the following steps:

1. Define the objectives: The first step in developing a stress-testing framework is to define the objectives of the exercise. This could include identifying potential risks in the portfolio, understanding the potential impact of various market or economic scenarios, or meeting regulatory requirements.

2. Define the scenarios: The next step is to define the stress scenarios that the portfolio will be tested against. Stress sce-

narios should be designed to reflect events that are plausible but
unlikely, and should consider a range of economic and market
variables that could impact the portfolio.

3. Define the modeling approach: The third step is to define
the modeling approach that will be used to estimate the impact of the stress scenarios on the portfolio. This may involve
developing statistical models, using historical data to estimate
the impact of past events, or using third-party models.

4. Conduct the stress tests: Once the scenarios, modeling approach, and assumptions have been defined, the stress testing
can be conducted. This involves running the portfolio through
the stress scenarios and estimating the impact on key risk metrics such as value-at-risk (VaR), expected shortfall (ES), or
stress losses.

5. Evaluate the results: The final step is to evaluate the results
of the stress tests and use them to inform risk management
decisions. This may include adjusting the portfolio's risk profile, hedging against potential losses, or developing contingency
plans to respond to adverse events.

Example:

Suppose we want to stress test a portfolio of stocks against a
market downturn. We could define a stress scenario where the
stock market experiences a significant drop, leading to a decline
in the value of the portfolio. We might define this scenario in
terms of the S&P 500, assuming a 20% decline in the index over
a six-month period.

To model the impact of this scenario on the portfolio, we could
develop statistical models that estimate the relationship be-

tween the performance of the portfolio and the performance of
the S&P 500. We might also use historical data to estimate the
impact of past market downturns on the portfolio.

Once the models are developed, we would run the portfolio
through the stress scenario, estimating the impact on key risk
metrics such as VaR or ES. We could then use these results to
inform risk management decisions, such as adjusting the portfolio's asset allocation, hedging against potential losses, or developing contingency plans to respond to adverse events.

5.15   Can you discuss the impact of mar-
ket regulations, such as MiFID II, on
the field of quantitative finance?

Market regulations such as MiFID II can have a significant
impact on the field of quantitative finance. MiFID II (Markets in Financial Instruments Directive II) was implemented in
Europe in 2018, with the aim of increasing transparency and
investor protection in financial markets. Specifically, MiFID II
introduces new requirements for pre-trade and post-trade transparency, as well as stricter rules around best execution.

One of the potential impacts of MiFID II on quantitative finance is that it may shift trading volumes toward more transparent markets. The pre-trade transparency requirements mean
that market participants must report certain information about
their orders before executing them, which can increase transparency and reduce information asymmetry in the market. This
can potentially lead to increased trading in more transparent
markets, such as lit exchanges, as investors and traders seek to

access this additional information.

Another potential impact of MiFID II on quantitative finance is that it may change the way that market data is used and analyzed. With increased transparency and more data being reported, there may be opportunities for more sophisticated quantitative analysis of market trends and behavior. For example, traders may be able to use machine learning algorithms to analyze more granular data on order flows and trading activity, with the aim of identifying trading signals and predicting market movements.

MiFID II may also lead to changes in the way that investment products are structured and traded. For example, the new rules on best execution mean that brokers must take all sufficient steps to obtain the best possible result for their clients when executing orders. This may incentivize brokers to offer new types of trading services, such as smart order routing algorithms, which can help to optimize execution quality and minimize trading costs.

Overall, the impact of market regulations such as MiFID II on quantitative finance will depend on a range of factors, including the specifics of the regulation, the behavior of market participants, and the development of new quantitative techniques and technologies. However, it is clear that regulatory changes can have a significant impact on financial markets, and that the field of quantitative finance will need to continue to adapt and evolve to respond to these changes.

5.16 How do you manage the trade-off between model complexity and interpretability in quantitative finance?

The trade-off between model complexity and interpretability is a fundamental issue in quantitative finance. On one hand, a complex model may fit the data better and potentially provide better predictions. On the other hand, a simpler model may be easier to interpret and explain, which can be valuable in certain applications, such as regulatory reporting or risk management.

One approach to managing this trade-off is to use a hierarchy of models, where simpler models are nested within more complex ones. For example, a simple linear regression model can be nested within a more complex nonlinear regression model. The nested models can be compared using information criteria, such as the Akaike information criterion (AIC) or the Bayesian information criterion (BIC), which trade off goodness of fit and model complexity. This approach allows for flexibility in modeling while still maintaining interpretability.

Another approach is to use interpretable models from the outset, such as decision trees or linear regression. These models are easy to interpret and provide insights into the relationship between inputs and outputs. For example, a decision tree can be used to identify the most important features for predicting a certain outcome, such as whether a customer will default on a loan. These insights can be used to inform decision making and improve the transparency of the model.

In addition, feature selection and regularization techniques can be used to reduce the complexity of models while still maintaining their predictive power. Feature selection involves selecting a subset of the available features that are most predictive of the outcome, while regularization involves adding a penalty term to the model's objective function to discourage overfitting. For example, lasso regularization can be used to encourage sparsity in a linear regression model, by adding a penalty proportional to the sum of the absolute values of the coefficients.

Ultimately, the choice of model complexity should be driven by the goals of the project and the available data. In some cases, a complex model may be necessary to capture the nuances of the data and make accurate predictions. In other cases, a simpler model may be more appropriate, particularly when the goal is to provide transparency and explainability to stakeholders. Choosing the appropriate level of model complexity requires a good understanding of the data, the modeling techniques, and the needs of the end user.

5.17 What are the main applications of natural language processing (NLP) techniques in the analysis of financial data?

Natural Language Processing (NLP) techniques have become increasingly important for the analysis of financial data. The applications of NLP techniques in the financial industry are numerous, and I will highlight some of the main ones below:

1. Sentiment analysis: Sentiment analysis aims to analyze the subjective information contained in natural language data to determine the sentiment of the writer. In finance, sentiment analysis can be used to analyze news articles, social media data,

and earnings call transcripts to determine the sentiment of investors regarding a particular stock or market. For example, positive sentiments in news articles related to a company could indicate that the company is performing well in the market, which could lead to an increase in stock prices.

2. Information extraction: NLP techniques can be used to extract specific financial or business-related information from textual data. This technique can be used to analyze financial statements or news articles to extract key financial indicators such as revenue, profit, or margin. This information can be used to make financial forecasts, identify investment opportunities, and automate financial analysis.

3. Document classification: Document classification involves categorizing documents based on their content. In finance, document classification can be used to categorize news articles or research papers based on their topics or industries. For example, an investment firm could use document classification to identify articles that are related to a particular industry, such as healthcare or technology, to obtain insights for investment decisions.

4. Summarization: NLP techniques can be used to automatically summarize financial reports or news articles, thus saving time and resources. A summary of a financial report could be useful to investors who do not have the time or expertise to read through the entire report.

5. Named entity recognition: Named entity recognition (NER) involves identifying and classifying named entities such as people, companies, or locations in textual data. In finance, NER can be used to identify the companies or individuals mentioned in news articles or social media data. This information can

be useful for investment analysis, detecting potential fraud, or monitoring corporate news.

In conclusion, NLP techniques have numerous applications in the financial industry that can help improve financial analysis, decision making, and automate tedious tasks.

5.18   Can you discuss the key advancements in high-performance computing and their implications for quantitative finance?

High-performance computing (HPC) has been a key enabler for the development of quantitative finance, providing the computational power necessary for complex and computationally-intensive financial modeling and analysis. In recent years, there have been several key advancements in HPC, including improvements in hardware, software, and algorithmic techniques, all of which have significant implications for quantitative finance. Some of the key advancements in HPC and their implications for quantitative finance are discussed below.

1. Hardware advancements: One of the most significant advancements in HPC has been the development of specialized hardware, such as graphics processing units (GPUs) and field-programmable gate arrays (FPGAs), which are specifically designed for parallel processing. These hardware advancements have significantly accelerated the pace of financial simulations, allowing for the execution of simulations faster than ever before. For example, while traditional CPUs may take months to complete a financial simulation, a simulation executed on a

GPU can be completed in just a few hours, or even minutes.

2. Software advancements: Another major advancement in HPC has been the development of software frameworks that can effectively harness the power of specialized hardware. One such framework is CUDA, which allows developers to write programs that can execute on GPUs. Another important framework is OpenCL, a cross-platform framework that allows developers to write programs that can execute on both CPUs and GPUs. These software advancements have made it possible to execute computationally-intensive financial models on specialized hardware, improving the speed and accuracy of financial simulations.

3. Algorithmic advancements: In addition to hardware and software advancements, there have been several important algorithmic advancements that have improved the performance of financial simulations. One such advancement is the use of Monte Carlo methods, which simulate complex financial processes by generating a large number of random samples. Another important algorithmic advancement is the use of parallel processing techniques, which enable multiple computations to be executed simultaneously across multiple processors, improving the overall speed of the simulation.

The implications of these HPC advancements for quantitative finance are significant. For example, they have made it possible to perform more complex financial simulations than ever before, enabling improved risk management practices and better-informed decision-making. They have also made it possible for financial institutions to process large amounts of data quickly and accurately, improving the speed and efficiency of their operations. Additionally, they have enabled the development of high-frequency trading algorithms, which can execute trades in fractions of a second, allowing traders to respond quickly to changing market conditions.

Overall, the advancements in HPC have been a game-changer for quantitative finance, providing the computational power necessary for complex financial modeling and analysis. As hardware, software, and algorithmic advancements continue to evolve, it is likely that even more sophisticated financial simulations will be possible, enabling improved financial decision-making and risk management practices.

5.19 How do you manage the risks associated with overfitting and model instability in quantitative finance?

Overfitting and model instability are challenges faced by quantitative finance professionals when building predictive models. Overfitting arises when a model performs well on the training data but poorly on new, unseen data. Model instability refers to the vulnerability of a model's ability to make accurate predictions due to variations in the input data. Here are some strategies for mitigating overfitting and model instability in quantitative finance:

1. Cross-validation: Cross-validation is a technique for assessing the performance of a model on new, unseen data. It involves dividing the data into training and test sets and evaluating the model's performance on the test set. Cross-validation allows the modeler to determine whether the model is overfitting the training data and to adjust the model accordingly.

2. Regularization: Regularization is a technique where a penalty term is added to the objective function of the model to discourage complex models. In essence, it shrinks the values of the model's parameters towards zero, reducing model complexity. L1 and L2 regularization are popular techniques in finance. In L1 regularization, the model penalty is proportional to the sum of the absolute values of the model parameters, whereas in L2 regularization, the model penalty is proportional to the square of the sums of the model parameters.

3. Ensemble techniques: Ensemble models combine multiple models to improve performance and reduce overfitting. A common example of an ensemble model is the random forest, which creates multiple decision trees and combines their predictions. By combining multiple models that overfit differently, the ensemble gets an overall view that is less prone to overfitting.

4. Robustness checks: Robustness checks involve testing the sensitivity of a model's predictions to variations in the input data. This technique can help identify unstable models and factors that may be leading to instability.

5. Dimensionality reduction: Dimensionality reduction techniques, such as principal component analysis (PCA) or factor analysis, can be used to identify and remove redundant variables that may lead to overfitting. By reducing the number of variables in a model, dimensionality reduction can help reduce model instability.

In summary, overfitting and model instability are risks that must be managed when building predictive models in quantitative finance. Techniques such as cross-validation, regularization, ensemble methods, robustness checks, and dimensionality reduction can all help mitigate these risks. Ultimately, model selection and tuning is a difficult endeavor that requires a deep understanding of the underlying data and phenomena, and practitioners must remain vigilant in monitoring and responding to model outputs, both as a means of recovering from instability, and as a way of identifying future opportunities for model improvement.

5.20   Can you discuss the role of environmental, social, and governance (ESG) factors in quantitative investment strategies and risk management?

Environmental, social, and governance (ESG) factors have become increasingly important in investment decision-making and risk management over the past few years. This is particularly true for quantitative investment strategies, which rely heavily on data-driven models and analytical techniques to identify and capture investment opportunities.

One of the main ways that ESG factors can be incorporated into quantitative investment strategies is through the use of ESG scores or ratings. These scores are typically based on a variety of metrics related to environmental impact, social responsibility, and corporate governance practices. For example, an ESG score might take into account a company's carbon footprint, diversity and inclusion policies, and board composition and structure.

These scores can then be used as inputs to quantitative models that seek to identify mispricings or opportunities in financial markets. For example, a model might identify companies with strong ESG scores as being undervalued relative to their peers, and therefore good candidates for investment. Alternatively, a model might use ESG scores as part of a risk management framework, seeking to avoid companies with poor ESG scores that could be more susceptible to negative events such as regulatory changes or reputational damage.

In addition to using ESG scores as inputs to quantitative models, there are also a number of more sophisticated quantitative techniques that can be employed to analyze and manage ESG-related risks. For example, machine learning algorithms can be used to uncover hidden patterns and relationships in ESG data, helping investors to identify potential risks or opportunities that may be difficult to detect using traditional methods. Similarly, natural language processing (NLP) techniques can be used to analyze large volumes of unstructured data such as news articles or social media posts, providing insight into how the market is perceiving ESG risks and opportunities.

Overall, the incorporation of ESG factors into quantitative investment strategies and risk management frameworks is becoming increasingly important as investors seek to align their portfolios with their values and manage a wider range of risks. While there are still challenges and limitations associated with the use of ESG data in quantitative models, advances in technology and data analytics are helping to overcome some of these barriers and facilitate more informed decision-making.

Chapter 6

Guru

6.1 Can you discuss the implications of agent-based modeling in understanding complex financial markets and systemic risk?

Agent-based modeling (ABM) is a computational approach used to simulate the behavior of individual agents and their interactions within a system. In finance, ABM has been used to understand complex financial markets and systemic risk by examining how individual market participants and their behavior may affect the larger system.

One of the key benefits of ABM is the ability to model heterogeneity among market participants. This means that agents within the model can have different characteristics, objectives, and strategies. For example, some agents may be risk-averse, while others may be more risk-seeking. By allowing for such heterogeneity, ABMs can simulate a more realistic market environment and capture different types of behavior that can affect prices and systemic risk.

Another benefit of ABM is the ability to model feedback loops and nonlinearities within the system. These can arise in financial markets when individual actions can affect other market participants, leading to a chain reaction of feedback loops that can amplify small shocks and lead to systemic risk. By simulating the behavior of individual agents and their interactions, ABMs can capture these nonlinearities and provide insight into how systemic risk can arise.

ABMs can also be used to explore the impact of different policies on financial markets and systemic risk. For example, one can use an ABM to simulate the impact of a new regulatory policy on individual agents and the market as a whole. By experimenting with different policies and their impact on the system, policymakers can gain a better understanding of the potential consequences of different regulatory initiatives.

Overall, ABMs offer a powerful tool for understanding the behavior of financial markets and systemic risk. However, they also come with certain limitations, such as the difficulty of calibrating model parameters and the complexity of interpreting model results. As with any modeling approach, ABMs should be applied with caution and their results should be interpreted in conjunction with other empirical and theoretical evidence.

6.2 How do you address the challenges of non-stationarity and long-range dependence in financial time series analysis?

Financial time series analysis poses significant challenges due to the presence of non-stationarity and long-range dependence. These two characteristics are often observed in financial data and need to be accounted for in any statistical analysis to avoid spurious results.

Non-stationarity refers to the fact that key statistical properties of a time series, such as mean and variance, change over time, making it difficult to model the series using traditional stationary models. This concept is particularly relevant in the financial world, where market conditions are continuously evolving, leading to non-stationary returns. To address non-stationarity, one can either transform a non-stationary time series into a stationary form through differencing, or use models specifically designed to handle non-stationary data, such as autoregressive integrated moving average (ARIMA) or autoregressive conditional heteroskedasticity (ARCH) models.

Long-range dependence refers to the persistence of shocks or volatility in a time series beyond what is expected in stationary processes. This means that a shock or volatility event can have a lasting impact on future observations. In finance, the long-range dependence is often generated by the high degree of interdependence among financial markets due to global factors such as political and economic events. To address this challenge, one can use models that account for long-range dependence, such as the autoregressive fractionally integrated moving average (ARFIMA) or fractional stochastic volatility (FSV) models.

Here is an example of how to address non-stationarity and long-range dependence in financial time series analysis using Python:

```python
import pandas as pd
import numpy as np
from statsmodels.tsa.arima_process import ArmaProcess
from statsmodels.tsa.arima_model import ARIMA

# generate non-stationary time series
np.random.seed(123)
ar3 = np.array([1, -0.8, 0.2, -0.1])
ma3 = np.array([1, 0.5, 0.2, 0.1])
ar3ma3 = ArmaProcess(ar3, ma3)
nonstationary_series = ar3ma3.generate_sample(nsample=100)

# transform non-stationary series into stationary form
stationary_series = np.diff(nonstationary_series)

# fit ARIMA model to stationary series
model = ARIMA(stationary_series, order=(1, 1, 1))
results = model.fit()

# generate long-range dependent time series using FSV
from arch import arch_model
np.random.seed(123)
sigma = 0.1 + 0.8*np.abs(np.random.randn(1000))
epsilon = sigma*np.random.randn(1000)
y = np.cumsum(epsilon)

# fit FSV model to long-range dependent series
model = arch_model(y, vol='fsv', p=1, o=1, q=1, dist='normal')
results = model.fit()
```

In this example, we first generated a non-stationary time series using an ARMA process with non-zero mean. We then transformed this series into a stationary form using differencing and fitted an ARIMA model to the stationary series. This approach enables us to analyze the stationary part of the series without being affected by non-stationarity. We then generated a long-range dependent time series using a fractional stochastic volatility (FSV) model and fitted an FSV model to the data. This approach accounts for long-range dependence, which allows us to capture the volatility clustering and persistence observed in the financial data.

6.3 Can you discuss the advancements in the field of artificial intelligence (AI) and their potential impact on the future of quantitative finance?

The field of artificial intelligence (AI) has seen significant advancements in recent years, which have already impacted various industries, including the finance industry. In quantitative finance, AI has the potential to significantly alter the way financial models are built, implemented, and used for data analysis and decision-making. Here are some of the advancements in AI and their potential impact on quantitative finance.

1. Machine Learning (ML):

Machine learning is a subset of AI that involves training algorithms to learn from data and make predictions or decisions based on that data. In quantitative finance, machine learning can be used to develop predictive models that can discern patterns or anomalies in financial data, assess credit risk, identify market trends, and more. For example, machine learning algorithms can be used to analyze trading data to identify the most profitable trading strategies or to make predictions about future investment returns.

2. Natural Language Processing (NLP):

Natural language processing is a branch of AI that deals with the interaction between computers and human languages. In finance, NLP technology can be used to analyze financial news and reports, social media, regulatory filings, and other sources of information to make better investment decisions. It can also be used to detect fraud, identify emerging risks, or monitor market sentiment.

3. Deep Learning:

Deep learning is a type of machine learning that uses artificial neural networks to model complex and nonlinear relationships between inputs and outputs. In finance, deep learning can be used to develop predictive models that can identify market trends, forecast asset prices, and predict market volatility or risk. For example, deep learning algorithms can be used to analyze large datasets of financial time series to identify patterns and relationships that are not apparent through traditional statistical methods.

4. Reinforcement Learning:

Reinforcement learning is a type of machine learning that involves an algorithm learning to make decisions by trial-and-error. In finance, reinforcement learning can be used to develop trading systems that learn and adapt to changing market conditions. For example, reinforcement learning algorithms can be used to optimize portfolio strategies by learning from past decisions and outcomes.

Overall, these advancements in AI have the potential to revolutionize the way quantitative finance is done, and there are already some notable examples of their impact. For instance, hedge funds like Renaissance Technologies and Two Sigma have been using machine learning and AI algorithms for years, and they have achieved significant success. However, there are also some challenges associated with AI in finance, such as data quality issues, interpretability of algorithms, and risks related to model accuracy and stability. Therefore, it is crucial to approach AI in finance with caution, and enhancements must be made to data quality, governance, and model performance monitoring to ensure accurate and reproducible results.

6.4 What are the key considerations in the development of robust and adaptive trading strategies in the context of evolving market dynamics?

The development of robust and adaptive trading strategies in the context of evolving market dynamics requires careful consideration of several key factors. In this answer, we will discuss some of these considerations.

1. Statistical analysis: The first step in developing any trading strategy is to perform a thorough statistical analysis of the relevant financial markets. This analysis should consider factors such as volatility, trendiness, seasonality, and correlations between assets. Understanding these statistical properties of the market is critical for developing strategies that are robust to changing market conditions.

2. Risk management: Any trading strategy must also include effective risk management techniques. This can include measures such as stop-loss orders, position sizing, and diversification. These techniques can help reduce exposure to potential losses and increase the probability of long-term profitability.

3. Machine learning techniques: Machine learning techniques offer a powerful way to develop adaptive trading strategies. By training models on historical data, machine learning algorithms can identify patterns in market dynamics and generate predictions about future trends. These predictions can then be used to optimize trading strategies and make real-time decisions.

4. Optimization techniques: Given the complexity of financial markets, it is often necessary to use optimization techniques to develop effective trading strategies. This can include techniques such as genetic algorithms, simulated annealing, and particle swarm optimization. These techniques can help identify optimal trading parameters and reduce the risk of overfitting to historical data.

5. Backtesting: Before deploying any trading strategy in real-world markets, it is critical to perform extensive backtesting. Backtesting involves applying the trading strategy to historical data to evaluate its performance in different market conditions. Backtesting enables traders to assess the robustness and adaptiveness of the strategy and identify areas for improvement.

6. Market monitoring: Finally, any trading strategy must be regularly monitored and adjusted to reflect changing market conditions. This requires ongoing data analysis and model refinement to ensure that the strategy remains effective over time. Effective market monitoring can help traders stay ahead of the curve and identify new opportunities for profit.

Overall, developing robust and adaptive trading strategies is a complex and multifaceted process that requires careful consideration of many factors. However, by following best practices such as those outlined above, traders can increase their chances of generating long-term profits in today's dynamic financial markets.

6.5 How do you address the impact of market frictions and transaction costs in the development of high-frequency trading strategies?

Market frictions and transaction costs are critical factors that need to be considered while developing high-frequency trading strategies. High-frequency trading involves executing a large number of trades within a short period, often milliseconds. In such a scenario, even minor market frictions and transaction costs can have a significant impact on the profitability of the trading strategy.

Market frictions refer to factors that affect the liquidity and efficiency of the market, such as bid-ask spreads, order imbalances, market impact, and price impact. Transaction costs, on the other hand, are the costs associated with executing the trades, including commissions, fees, and slippage.

To address the impact of market frictions and transaction costs, traders often use specialized techniques and models. Here are some examples:

1. Optimal order execution: This technique aims to minimize transaction costs by optimizing the execution of trades. It involves modeling the impact of trades on the market and determining the optimal size, timing, and sequencing of orders to minimize the costs.

2. Market microstructure models: These models capture the dynamics of the market and account for market frictions such as bid-ask spreads, liquidity, and order imbalances. They can be used to estimate transaction costs and adjust the trading strategy accordingly.

3. Statistical arbitrage: Statistical arbitrage is a trading strategy that takes advantage of price differentials between related securities. To account for market frictions and transaction costs, the strategy involves using statistical models to estimate the trading costs and adjust the positions accordingly.

4. Pairs trading: Pairs trading is a market-neutral strategy that involves taking long and short positions in two highly correlated securities. Transaction costs and market frictions can be minimized by optimizing the size and timing of the trades and using statistical models to estimate the costs.

5. Machine learning algorithms: Machine learning algorithms can be used to analyze market data and identify patterns that can be used to reduce transaction costs and account for market frictions.

Overall, it is crucial to carefully consider the impact of market frictions and transaction costs while developing high-frequency trading strategies. The use of specialized techniques and models can help traders optimize their trading strategies and improve profitability.

6.6   Can you discuss the role of advanced optimization techniques, such as genetic algorithms and simulated annealing, in portfolio management and strategy development?

Optimization techniques play a crucial role in portfolio management and strategy development. Optimization procedures are designed in such a way that we can measure the risk-reward trade-off of alternative investment opportunities and create optimally diversified portfolios. In recent years, advances in computing have made it easier to use more sophisticated optimization techniques, such as genetic algorithms and simulated annealing. These optimization techniques can be used to refine a vast search space and identify optimal portfolios in the presence of constraints.

Genetic algorithms are a type of optimization technique used to solve complex problems by mimicking the process of natural selection. They work by combining genetic operators, such as mutation and crossover, on a set of potential solutions. For portfolio optimization, genetic algorithms can be used to simultaneously optimize asset allocation while incorporating portfolio constraints such as maximum portfolio weights or minimum holdings. These algorithms provide a mechanism for exploring the entire solution space to identify an optimized portfolio. One key advantage of genetic algorithms is that they can be calibrated to explore a high-dimensional solution space with many possible asset combinations. Furthermore, genetic algorithms allow for not just one, but multiple optimal solutions which enables the investors to choose the best one suited to their preferences.

Simulated annealing is another optimization technique that is commonly used in portfolio management. It is a stochastic global optimization algorithm that simulates the physical annealing process of slowly cooling molten metal to find the global optimum for a given function. Simulated annealing can be used to solve problems in which the fitness landscape is complex and has many local optima. Within portfolio optimization a cost function is created, which quantifies the risk and return tradeoff of an investment opportunity. Simulated annealing can then be used to search for the optimal allocation of assets by computing the solution that maximizes this cost function while exploring the entire search space.

Both genetic algorithms and simulated annealing have shown impressive results in the portfolio optimization literature, having been applied and tested on various financial datasets. Moreover, these techniques allow for the optimization of portfolios that incorporate a diverse range of asset classes and constraints, such as transaction costs or policy restrictions. As such, they provide a valuable tool for portfolio managers and investors looking to optimize and diversify their portfolios.

6.7 What are the main challenges and advancements in the field of credit risk modeling and management, particularly in the context of systemic risk and contagion?

Credit risk modeling and management have always been crucial areas for financial institutions to ensure their stability and continued success. However, since the financial crisis of 2008, the importance of credit risk management in the context of systemic risk and contagion has become even more evident. In this answer, I will discuss some of the main challenges and advancements in the field of credit risk modeling and management within this context.

One of the main challenges in credit risk modeling and management is identifying and quantifying systemic risk and contagion effects. Systemic risk refers to the risk of a financial system-wide collapse, while contagion refers to the spread of credit risk from one market to another. Both are difficult to model due to the complex relationships and feedback loops between institutions, markets, and economies. In addition, there is often incomplete and asymmetrical information available which can make it difficult to accurately assess the potential impact of default events.

To address these challenges, there have been several advancements in credit risk modeling and management. One approach is to use network analysis to model the relationships between different institutions and markets. This can help identify potential sources of systemic risk and contagion effects. For example, if a particular institution has high levels of exposure to other institutions, a default event could disrupt the entire network. By identifying these key players and their relationships, institutions can take steps to mitigate their exposure to systemic risk and contagion effects.

Another approach is to use machine learning and big data analytics to improve credit risk management. These techniques can be applied to a wide range of data sources, such as financial statements, economic indicators, and news articles, to identify potential credit risk and predict default events. For example, sentiment analysis can be used to analyze news articles and social media posts to identify potential negative events or rumors that could impact an institution's credit risk. By incorporating these types of data into credit risk models, institutions can better assess their exposure to systemic risk and contagion effects.

Finally, regulators have also implemented new regulations and guidelines to improve credit risk management and mitigate systemic risk and contagion effects. For example, the Basel III framework includes requirements for minimum capital ratios and stress testing to ensure institutions are able to withstand potential default events. In addition, regulators are also requiring institutions to improve their data management and reporting systems to better assess and manage their exposure to credit risk.

In summary, credit risk modeling and management within the context of systemic risk and contagion remain challenging due to the complex relationships and feedback loops between institutions and markets. However, advancements in network analysis, machine learning, and data analytics, along with regulatory reforms, are improving our ability to identify and manage credit risk and mitigate the potential impact of default events on the financial system as a whole.

6.8 Can you discuss the limitations of traditional risk metrics, such as VaR and CVaR, and explore alternative risk measures that better capture tail risk and extreme events?

Value at Risk (VaR) and Conditional Value at Risk (CVaR) are traditional risk metrics that have become the industry standard over the last few decades. VaR is defined as the maximum potential loss in a portfolio over a specified time horizon at a certain level of confidence. It measures only the worst-case scenario of portfolio losses and assumes normally distributed returns. CVaR, on the other hand, measures expected losses beyond VaR and provides information on the magnitude of potential losses as well as their frequency.

While VaR and CVaR have proven to be useful tools for risk measurement, they are not without limitations. One of the most significant is the fact that they are not robust to model misspecification. They rely on the assumption that asset returns are normally distributed, which is often violated in practice, especially during extreme events or tail risk.

Furthermore, VaR is a non-convex risk measure, meaning it cannot accurately capture non-linear risk, such as optionality or convexity. It does not provide any information on the shape of the tail distribution of losses, nor does it distinguish between left and right tails. CVaR, however, provides information on tail risk, but it is still not always sufficient to capture extreme events.

As a result, several alternative risk measures have been developed to better capture tail risk and extreme events. Among them are:

1. Expected Shortfall (ES) – also known as Tail VaR, this measure provides information on the expected value of losses beyond a certain level of VaR. It is robust to model misspecification and can capture non-linear risk.

$$ES_\alpha = -E[R|R \leq -VaR_\alpha]$$

2. Spectral Risk Measures – these measures involve the decomposition of the distribution of losses, which allows for the evaluation of extreme events and tail risk from different perspectives.

3. Coherent Risk Measures – these measures satisfy certain axioms, such as sub-additivity, and are typically more flexible and robust than VaR and CVaR. Examples include Expected Utility, Mean-Variance, and Entropic Value at Risk.

In summary, while VaR and CVaR have been widely used and accepted as standard risk metrics, they do have limitations in their ability to capture tail risk and extreme events. Alternative risk measures, such as ES, spectral risk measures, and coherent risk measures, offer more flexibility and robustness to model misspecification and non-linear risk. It is important for risk managers to understand these limitations and consider alternative measures when assessing the risk in their portfolios.

6.9 How do you address the challenges of integrating sentiment analysis, news analytics, and social media data into quantitative models for improved forecasting and decision-making?

Integrating sentiment analysis, news analytics, and social media data into quantitative models can improve the forecasting and decision-making process by providing timely and relevant information about public opinion, events, and trends. However, there are several challenges that need to be addressed to ensure that the resulting models are accurate, robust, and informative.

One of the main challenges is data quality. Sentiment analysis, news analytics, and social media data are often noisy, unstructured, and biased, which can affect the performance of the models. For example, social media platforms can be prone to fake news or misinformation, and sentiment analysis tools may not accurately capture the nuances of human emotions. To address this challenge, it is essential to employ robust data preprocessing and cleaning techniques to filter out irrelevant or misleading data points and ensure that the remaining data is representative and informative.

Another challenge is feature selection and extraction. Sentiment analysis, news analytics, and social media data typically have a large number of features, which can make it challenging to identify the most relevant and informative ones for the model. Feature selection techniques such as principal component analysis (PCA) and correlation analysis can be used to reduce the dimensionality of the data and identify the most important features. Feature extraction techniques such as latent semantic analysis (LSA) and topic modeling can also be used to extract meaningful information from the data.

A third challenge is model selection and validation. There are several quantitative models that can be used to analyze senti- ment, news analytics, and social media data, including regres- sion models, time series models, and machine learning models such as random forests, support vector machines (SVM), and neural networks. Choosing the right model is essential to ensure that the model is accurate, robust, and interpretable. Model validation techniques such as cross-validation, backtesting, and out-of-sample testing can be used to assess the performance of the model and ensure that it is not overfitting.

In addition to these challenges, it is also essential to consider the ethical and legal implications of integrating sentiment anal- ysis, news analytics, and social media data into quantitative models. Privacy concerns, bias, and discrimination are some of the potential risks that need to be addressed to ensure that the models are fair and transparent.

To illustrate the integration of sentiment analysis, news ana- lytics, and social media data into quantitative models, consider the following example. Suppose we are interested in predict- ing the stock price of a company based on social media data, news articles, and sentiment analysis. We can collect data from various sources, preprocess and clean the data, extract relevant features, and use a machine learning model such as an SVM to train the model. We can then validate the model using cross- validation and out-of-sample testing and assess its performance. If the model is accurate and robust, we can use it to make in- formed decisions about investing in the company.

6.10 Can you discuss the role of network theory in understanding the interconnectedness of financial markets and the propagation of risk across market participants?

Network theory, also known as graph theory, provides a powerful framework for understanding the complex relationships and interactions between financial market participants. In a financial context, network theory can help us understand the structure of connections between different financial institutions and how these connections influence risk propagation.

Central to network theory is the concept of a network, which is a collection of nodes (also called vertices) that are connected by edges (also called links or edges). In a financial network, each node represents a financial institution, and each edge represents a financial relationship or transaction between two institutions. By analyzing the structure of a financial network, we can gain insights into the way that risk spreads through interbank lending and other types of financial transactions.

For example, consider a simple network of three banks, A, B and C, where A has lent money to B, and B has lent money to C. In this network, if bank C were to suddenly become insolvent and default on its loans, this would have an impact not only on B, but also on A because its borrower, B, is now in trouble. This situation is known as counterparty risk, and it can propagate quickly through a tightly interconnected network of financial institutions, potentially leading to a systemic crisis.

Network theory can also help us understand the role of different financial institutions in the propagation of risk. For example, some institutions may have a large number of connections to other institutions, making them more central in the network and potentially more influential in transmitting risk. These institutions are known as systemically important financial institutions (SIFIs). Understanding the importance of SIFIs in a financial network is crucial for regulators and policymakers, who must consider the potential impact of policy changes on the stability of the entire financial system.

In addition to understanding the propagation of risk through financial networks, network theory can also be used to identify patterns and anomalies in financial data. For example, network analysis can be used to identify clusters of financial institutions that behave similarly or to identify outliers that may be particularly vulnerable to risk.

Overall, network theory provides a powerful framework for understanding the complex relationships and interactions between financial institutions, and it can help us identify potential sources of risk in the financial system. By using tools from network theory to analyze financial data, we can gain a deeper understanding of the interconnectedness of financial markets and the potential for risk propagation in times of stress.

6.11 How do you develop robust, adaptive, and interpretable machine learning models in the context of high-dimensional and noisy financial data?

Developing robust, adaptive, and interpretable machine learning models in the context of high-dimensional and noisy financial data requires carefully selecting the appropriate machine learning algorithms, preprocessing and feature engineering methods, model validation techniques, and interpretability tools.

Firstly, selecting the right machine learning algorithm is crucial. Ensemble methods such as Random Forest, Gradient Boosting and Extreme Gradient Boosting (XGBoost) are often used in finance due to their ability to handle noisy and high-dimensional data, as well as to handle class imbalance and overfitting. Another popular algorithm used in finance is Support Vector Machines (SVM), which is a powerful classification and regression technique, capable of handling non-linear data.

Secondly, preprocessing and feature engineering techniques play an important role in developing robust models. Dimensionality reduction techniques such as Principal Component Analysis (PCA) and feature selection methods such as Recursive Feature Elimination (RFE) can help to reduce the number of features, while at the same time retaining the most salient information. To handle noisy data, feature scaling methods like StandardScaler, MinMaxScaler, and RobustScaler may be used to normalize the data.

Thirdly, model validation techniques such as cross-validation

can help to avoid overfitting and estimate the robustness of the
model. It is important to use an appropriate metric such as
accuracy, precision, recall or F1-score to evaluate the model's
performance. Additionally, regularization methods such as L1
and L2 regularization can help to penalize complex models that
may overfit.

Lastly, interpretable machine learning techniques such as feature importance, shap values, partial dependence plots, per-
mutation importance, and LIME (Local Interpretable Model-
Agnostic Explanations) can help to understand how the model
is making predictions, and gain insights into the features that
drive the predictions.

For example, we can use XGBoost algorithm with PCA for
feature selection, StandardScaler for feature scaling, and cross-
validation for model validation. We can then use the permuta-
tion importance and shap values to interpret the model's predictions and gain insights into the most salient features.

```
# Import the required libraries
import pandas as pd
from sklearn.model_selection import train_test_split,
    cross_val_score
from sklearn.metrics import accuracy_score, classification_report,
    confusion_matrix
from sklearn.preprocessing import StandardScaler
from sklearn.decomposition import PCA
import xgboost as xgb
import shap
from sklearn.inspection import permutation_importance

# Load the data
df = pd.read_csv("financial_data.csv")

# Separate the features and target variables
X = df.drop('target', axis=1)
y = df['target']

# Split the data into training and testing sets
X_train, X_test, y_train, y_test = train_test_split(X, y, test_size
    =0.3, random_state=42)

# Scale the features using StandardScaler
sc = StandardScaler()
```

```
X_train = sc.fit_transform(X_train)
X_test = sc.transform(X_test)

# Apply PCA for feature selection
pca = PCA(n_components=10)
X_train = pca.fit_transform(X_train)
X_test = pca.transform(X_test)

# Train the XGBoost model using cross-validation
model = xgb.XGBClassifier()
scores = cross_val_score(model, X_train, y_train, cv=5)
print("Cross-validation scores:", scores)
print("Average cross-validation score:", scores.mean())

# Fit the model to the training data
model.fit(X_train, y_train)

# Make predictions on the test data
y_pred = model.predict(X_test)

# Evaluate the model's performance
print("Accuracy score:", accuracy_score(y_test, y_pred))
print(classification_report(y_test, y_pred))
print(confusion_matrix(y_test, y_pred))

# Use permutation importance to determine feature importance
perm_importance = permutation_importance(model, X_test, y_test)
sorted_idx = perm_importance.importances_mean.argsort()[::-1]
for i in sorted_idx:
     print(f"{X.columns[i]:<20}"
            f"{perm_importance.importances_mean[i]:.3f}"
            f" +/- {perm_importance.importances_std[i]:.3f}")

# Use shap values to explain the model's predictions
explainer = shap.Explainer(model)
shap_values = explainer(X_test)
shap.summary_plot(shap_values, X_test, plot_type="bar")

# Use partial dependence plots to visualize the effect of a feature
    on the predictions
pdp = pdpbox.pdp.pdp_isolate(model=model, dataset=X_test,
     model_features=X.columns, feature='feature_1')
pdpbox.pdp.pdp_plot(pdp, 'Feature 1')

# Use LIME to explain an individual prediction
explainer = LimeTabularExplainer(X_train, feature_names=X.columns,
     class_names=["negative", "positive"])
exp = explainer.explain_instance(X_test.iloc[0], model.predict_proba
     )
exp.show_in_notebook()
```

6.12   What are the main challenges and advancements in the field of market microstructure research, particularly with respect to liquidity and order flow dynamics?

Market microstructure research is concerned with understanding the process by which assets are traded in financial markets. The study of liquidity and order flow dynamics is one of the main focuses of market microstructure research. In this context, liquidity refers to the ease with which a financial instrument can be traded in a market without affecting the price of the instrument, while order flow refers to the direction and volume of trading activity in a market.

The main challenges in the field of market microstructure research include the complexity of financial markets, the lack of transparency, and the difficulty of obtaining high-quality data. Financial markets are highly complex systems in which the behavior of market participants is influenced by a wide range of factors, including market structure, regulation, and technology. Moreover, many financial markets are highly opaque, meaning that information about the state of the market and the behavior of other market participants is often limited. These challenges can make it difficult for researchers to develop accurate models of market behavior and to test these models empirically.

Despite these challenges, there have been several advancements in the field of market microstructure research in recent years. One of the most important advancements has been the development of high-frequency trading (HFT) algorithms, which use sophisticated mathematical models and computational algorithms to trade financial instruments at extremely high speeds. HFT has had a significant impact on market microstructure research, as it has increased the amount and quality of data available to researchers and has led to the development of new models for understanding market behavior.

Another important advancement in market microstructure research has been the development of agent-based models (ABMs). ABMs are models that simulate the behavior of individual market participants, such as traders and investors, and their interactions in a virtual market environment. ABMs can be used to test hypotheses about market behavior and to identify the key factors that influence market outcomes.

In terms of liquidity and order flow dynamics, one of the main challenges in market microstructure research has been the identification and modeling of liquidity shocks. Liquidity shocks are sudden changes in the demand for liquidity that can occur in financial markets due to a variety of factors, such as changes in market sentiment, regulatory changes, or financial crises. These shocks can have a significant impact on market prices and can lead to the emergence of contagion and systemic risk.

To address this challenge, researchers have developed a variety of models for predicting liquidity shocks and for measuring the resilience of financial markets to these shocks. For example, some researchers have developed models that use machine learning algorithms to predict the probability of a liquidity shock based on patterns in market data. Other researchers have used econometric models to estimate the susceptibility of financial markets to liquidity shocks and to identify the factors that make certain markets more susceptible than others.

Overall, the field of market microstructure research is a rapidly evolving and highly interdisciplinary field that is driven by advances in technology, data availability, and computational power. Despite the challenges inherent in studying complex financial systems, researchers continue to make important contributions to our understanding of liquidity and order flow dynamics in financial markets.

6.13   Can you discuss the implications of behavioral biases and heuristics on market efficiency and the development of novel trading strategies?

Behavioral biases and heuristics can have significant implications on market efficiency and the development of novel trading strategies because they can lead to market anomalies and inefficiencies. These anomalies and inefficiencies, in turn, can create opportunities for profit if exploited properly through the development of novel trading strategies.

Behavioral biases refer to the systematic errors in judgment or decision-making that individuals exhibit due to cognitive constraints, emotions, or social norms. Heuristics, on the other hand, are mental shortcuts or rules of thumb that individuals use to simplify decision-making. These biases and heuristics can impact market efficiency through several mechanisms.

Firstly, they can lead to information asymmetry, where certain market participants have access to information that others do not. For example, the confirmation bias, which is the tendency to seek out information that confirms pre-existing beliefs, can lead investors to overweight information that confirms their be-

liefs and underweight information that contradicts them, leading to information asymmetry. This information asymmetry
can create inefficiencies when the market fails to fully incorporate this information into stock prices, which can lead to profit
opportunities for those who are able to exploit them.

Secondly, biases and heuristics can create market anomalies,
where the market fails to follow rational expectations or pricing models. For example, the disposition effect, which is the
tendency to hold on to losing positions and sell winning ones,
has been shown to create abnormal returns in the stock market
by creating buying pressure for past losers and selling pressure
for past winners.

Thirdly, biases and heuristics can impact market liquidity, where
the supply and demand for securities are influenced by investor
sentiment and market conditions rather than fundamental values. For example, the herding behavior, where investors tend
to follow the actions of others in the market, can lead to large
movements in prices that are not justified by underlying fundamentals, leading to illiquidity.

The implications of these effects on market efficiency are twofold.
Firstly, they highlight the limitations of the efficient market hypothesis, which assumes that market participants act rationally
and that prices fully reflect all available information. Secondly,
they open up the possibility for developing novel trading strategies that can exploit these inefficiencies for profit. For example,
quantitative trading strategies that are based on statistical arbitrage or market microstructure can take advantage of market
inefficiencies caused by biases and heuristics.

In summary, behavioral biases and heuristics can have significant implications on market efficiency and the development of

novel trading strategies. By creating information asymmetry, market anomalies, and impacting market liquidity, they challenge the efficient market hypothesis and create profit opportunities for those who are able to exploit them.

6.14   What are the main considerations in the development of quantitative models for the pricing and risk management of complex, illiquid, and bespoke financial instruments?

The development of quantitative models for the pricing and risk management of complex, illiquid, and bespoke financial instruments is a challenging task that requires careful consideration of several factors. Here are some of the main considerations in the development of quantitative models for such instruments:

1. Market data: The availability and quality of market data is crucial for the development of quantitative models. For complex, illiquid, and bespoke financial instruments, market data may be scarce or non-existent. In such cases, the model developer may need to rely on other sources of information, such as historical data or expert judgment, to calibrate the model.

2. Model structure: The structure of the model is critical for pricing and risk management. For instance, some complex instruments may require Monte Carlo simulations, while others may require numerical methods, such as finite difference or finite element techniques. In either case, the model must accurately capture the relevant features of the instrument.

3. Model assumptions: The assumptions made in the model must be carefully considered and justified. For instance, the volatility of the underlying asset may be assumed to be constant or stochastic. The choice of assumptions will impact the accuracy of the model and the resulting prices and risk measures.

4. Calibration: Once the model structure and assumptions have been established, the model must be calibrated using market data or other information. This process involves adjusting model parameters to match observed market prices or other relevant data points. The accuracy of the calibration process is critical for the validity of the model.

5. Sensitivity analysis: Models for complex, illiquid, and bespoke financial instruments are often highly sensitive to changes in model inputs or assumptions. As such, it is essential to perform sensitivity analysis to assess the impact of these changes on the model outputs. This analysis is also critical for understanding the sources of model risk and for designing effective risk mitigation strategies.

6. Validation: The final stage in the development of quantitative models is validation. This involves testing the model on out-of-sample data or using other methods to assess its accuracy and robustness. The aim of validation is to ensure that the model is fit for purpose and that it provides reliable pricing and risk measures.

Example:

Consider a complex derivative of a commodity, such as a swing option on the price of crude oil. The swing option gives the holder the right, but not the obligation, to take a certain number of barrels of crude oil at any time during a specified period at a specified price. Such an instrument is complex, illiquid, and bespoke, as it depends on the fluctuation of the price of crude oil over a given period, which is uncertain.

The development of a quantitative model for pricing and risk management of this type of derivatives requires a careful consideration of the market data, model structure, and assumptions. The volatility of the price of crude oil may be assumed to be stochastic, and the model structure may involve a Monte Carlo simulation. The model assumptions might include the presence of seasonal patterns in the volatility of the oil price, which can be included in the model as a stochastic process.

The model must then be calibrated using a variety of data points, such as historical prices, market prices of similar instruments, and expert opinions. The calibration process is critical for ensuring the model's accuracy and reliability.

Once the model has been calibrated, sensitivity analysis must be performed to assess the model's sensitivity to changes in inputs and assumptions. For instance, changing the volatility assumptions or adjusting the correlation between the price of crude oil and other assets can have a significant impact on the pricing and risk measures.

Validation of the model is also critical to ensure that it is reliable and fit for purpose. Out-of-sample testing and stress testing can be used to assess the model's accuracy and robustness. The validation process must also consider the model's limitations and sources of risk. For instance, the model may be highly sensitive to parameter estimation or calibration errors, which can lead to significant model risk.

6.15   Can you discuss the role of alternative risk premia strategies in enhancing portfolio diversification and performance?

Alternative risk premia (ARP) strategies have gained popularity in recent years as a way to enhance portfolio diversification and performance. ARP refers to a set of investment strategies that aim to generate returns by exploiting various sources of risk premia across different asset classes, such as equities, fixed income, currencies, and commodities. The objective of ARP is to provide investors with an alternative source of returns that is not correlated with traditional asset classes, such as stocks and bonds.

ARP strategies are generally based on a quantitative approach that relies heavily on mathematical models and statistical analysis to identify and exploit market inefficiencies. These strategies typically involve investing in a range of long and short positions in different asset classes to capture a range of sources of risk premia.

The key benefits of ARP strategies include portfolio diversification and enhanced risk-adjusted returns. By investing in a range of different asset classes, ARP strategies can help to reduce portfolio concentration risk and provide investors with exposure to a broader range of investment opportunities. Moreover, since ARP strategies are designed to capture sources of returns that are not correlated with traditional asset classes, they can help to improve portfolio efficiency by reducing overall portfolio risk.

There are several different types of ARP strategies, each based on a different source of risk premia. For example, equity market neutral strategies aim to exploit market inefficiencies in stock prices by taking long and short positions in different stocks, while value strategies aim to capture the premium associated with buying undervalued stocks and shorting overvalued stocks. Other common ARP strategies include trend-following strategies, carry strategies, and volatility strategies.

To illustrate the potential benefits of ARP strategies, let us consider the case of a hypothetical portfolio consisting of 50% stocks and 50% bonds. This portfolio is likely to be highly concentrated in traditional asset classes and therefore may be exposed to significant downside risk if there is a sudden market downturn. By introducing an ARP strategy, such as a trend-following strategy, an investor may be able to reduce overall portfolio volatility and improve risk-adjusted returns. Moreover, since these strategies are designed to be uncorrelated with traditional asset classes, they may also help to reduce the risk of extreme market events.

Overall, ARP strategies can play an important role in enhancing portfolio diversification and performance. By providing exposure to a range of alternative sources of returns, ARP strategies can help to reduce portfolio concentration risk and improve risk-adjusted returns. However, investors should be aware that these strategies often involve more complex investment strategies and may be subject to higher fees and costs than traditional asset classes. As with all investment strategies, it is important to conduct a thorough analysis of the risks and benefits of ARP strategies before making any investment decisions.

6.16 How do you address the challenges of incorporating climate risk and ESG factors into quantitative models and investment strategies?

Incorporating climate risk and ESG factors into quantitative models and investment strategies can provide a more accurate picture of investment opportunities and potential risks in portfolios. However, it poses several challenges that need to be addressed.

1. Data availability: One of the major challenges of incorporating climate risk and ESG factors in quantitative models is the availability of reliable data. Climate data is often limited in its scope and quality, while ESG data is diverse and sometimes incomplete. Therefore, robust data collection and cleaning processes are required to ensure the data used in models is accurate and complete.

2. Model complexity: Incorporating climate risk and ESG factors in models requires a more sophisticated approach than traditional models. Climate risk and ESG factors can interact in complex ways, making it difficult to develop accurate models. This requires more data inputs and complex models that can be challenging to develop and maintain.

3. Lack of consensus: There is a lack of agreement on which ESG factors are material for investment decisions, making it a challenge to develop consistent and reliable models. Additionally, there is a lack of standardization in ESG data, which makes it difficult to compare data from different sources.

Despite these challenges, there are several ways to address them and incorporate climate risk and ESG factors into quantitative models and investment strategies:

1. Start with data quality: Good data quality is essential for meaningful analysis. Therefore, an initial focus on data quality should be a priority by validating sources, addressing discrepancies and enhancing data collection & cleaning processes.

2. Break down models into components: breaking down models into smaller components can provide more clarity on how climate risk and ESG factors interact with a specific investment or portfolio. This can help to develop more accurate models that can capture the interplay between climate and ESG factors.

3. Combine quantitative and qualitative approaches: In some cases the available data may not be sufficient to perform quantitative analysis. This is where qualitative information might be help. Analysts can combine quantitative analysis with ESG scoring systems or qualitative analysis by ESG experts.

4. Addressing Uncertainty: Climate risk and ESG factors can be uncertain and complex, and therefore models should account for multiple scenarios or be updated frequently. It is crucial to employ stochastic modelling to capture the market's feedback loops and regime switching behaviours.

In conclusion, incorporating climate risk and ESG factors into quantitative models and investment strategies presents several challenges, but these can be addressed with robust data quality, complex modelling approaches, paying attention to the materiality of factors, combining quantitative with qualitative analysis, and accounting for uncertainty.

6.17   What are the main advancements in the field of high-performance computing, big data analytics, and cloud-based infrastructure in the context of quantitative finance?

The field of quantitative finance has significantly evolved in recent years due to advancements in high-performance computing, big data analytics, and cloud-based infrastructure. In this answer, we will discuss some of the main advancements and their impact on the field.

High-Performance Computing

High-performance computing (HPC) refers to the use of powerful computers or computer clusters to perform complex calculations or simulations. In quantitative finance, HPC has enabled the analysis of large datasets and the optimization of complex financial models. Some of the main advancements in HPC that are relevant to quantitative finance include:

GPUs and Parallel Computing

Graphics Processing Units (GPUs) can perform many floating-point calculations in parallel, making them ideal for use in parallel computing for financial modeling, risk analysis, and trading. By leveraging parallel computing, complex financial simulations can be performed in a shorter time period compared to using traditional Central Processing Units (CPUs).

Quantum Computing

Quantum computing is an area of research that has the potential to significantly impact the field of quantitative finance in the future. Quantum computers use quantum states to perform calculations and can potentially solve problems much faster than traditional computers. While still in its early stages, quantum computing has been explored in various areas of finance, including option pricing and portfolio optimization.

Example

One example of high-performance computing in quantitative finance is the use of Monte Carlo simulations for option pricing. Monte Carlo simulations are used to model the random movements of financial assets and can be used to price options. The simulations require a large number of calculations, which can be performed faster by leveraging HPC. By using GPUs or parallel computing, a larger number of simulations can be performed in a shorter time period, allowing for more accurate option pricing.

Big Data Analytics

Big data analytics involves the analysis and interpretation of large and complex datasets. In quantitative finance, big data analytics is used to analyze financial data and identify patterns or trends that can inform investment decisions, risk management strategies, and trading strategies. Some of the main advancements in big data analytics relevant to quantitative finance include:

Machine Learning

Machine learning is a subset of artificial intelligence that involves the use of algorithms to learn patterns from data. In

finance, machine learning algorithms are used to analyze large
datasets and identify patterns that can inform investment decisions. Machine learning algorithms can also be used to improve
trading strategies, risk management, and fraud detection.

Data Visualization

Data visualization tools are used to visually represent complex
data in a way that is easy to understand. In finance, data
visualization tools are used to analyze financial data and com-
municate insights to stakeholders. By using interactive tools,
analysts can explore data in real-time and identify trends or
anomalies.

Example

One example of big data analytics in quantitative finance is
the use of machine learning algorithms to predict stock prices.
A machine learning algorithm can analyze large amounts of financial data, such as company financials, news articles, and
social media sentiment to make predictions about a stock's future price movements. By combining data from various sources,
analysts can develop more accurate predictions compared to
traditional financial models.

Cloud-Based Infrastructure

Cloud-based infrastructure refers to the use of cloud computing services to store and analyze data. In finance, cloud-based
infrastructure enables the processing of large datasets and the
ability to scale up or down computing power as needed. Some
of the main advancements in cloud-based infrastructure that
are relevant to quantitative finance include:

Containerization

Containerization is a technology that allows for the deployment of software applications in a lightweight and portable manner. In finance, containerization can help to ensure that applications are running in a consistent environment, regardless of the underlying infrastructure.

Serverless Computing

Serverless computing involves the use of cloud services to execute code without the need for dedicated servers. In finance, serverless computing can be used to perform large-scale data processing tasks, such as risk analysis, without the need for dedicated hardware.

Example

One example of cloud-based infrastructure in quantitative finance is the use of containerization to deploy financial models. By using containerization, financial models can be deployed in a consistent environment regardless of the underlying infrastructure. Additionally, by leveraging serverless computing, financial institutions can perform large-scale data processing tasks such as risk analysis without the need for dedicated hardware.

In conclusion, the advancements in HPC, big data analytics, and cloud-based infrastructure have significantly impacted the field of quantitative finance. By using these technologies, financial institutions can analyze and process large amounts of data faster and more accurately. As these technologies continue to evolve, they will further improve the accuracy and efficiency of financial models and investment strategies.

6.18   Can you discuss the ethical considerations and potential societal impacts of widespread adoption of AI-driven algorithmic trading strategies in financial markets?

The rapid development and increasing adoption of artificial intelligence (AI) techniques in algorithmic trading, combined with the speed and volume of trades facilitated by high-frequency trading (HFT), have brought visible impacts on financial markets while raising ethical concerns.

One ethical concern is that AI models might perpetuate existing biases in the financial industry or even amplify them. For example, if a historical data set used to train an AI model contains biased data, that model would likely replicate the biases in the data, and the trading decisions made based on the output from the model could inherit such biases. Additionally, if computerized trading is solely focused on speed and efficiency, it might overlook other important factors such as companies' long-term interests, social responsibility, and environmental impact, which could negatively impact the society in the long run.

Another consideration is the fairness of market access. AI-driven algorithmic trading requires vast computing resources and sophisticated software tools to operate successfully. Smaller firms or individuals without access to such resources may find themselves at a disadvantage. Furthermore, the lightning-fast execution of algorithmic trades may create unintended consequences, such as flash crashes or market manipulations.

The immense amount of data that AI models rely on to make

trading decisions also raises concerns about data privacy and security. The potential of sensitive financial information being compromised or used for insider trading could threaten market integrity.

Finally, the deployment of AI techniques in algorithmic trading inevitably raises the question of human autonomy and the disposal of job opportunities. While AI technology is powerful and enables rapid analysis of massive amounts of complex data, AI systems cannot entirely replicate human judgment and creativity in decision-making. Therefore, human involvement is still necessary in algorithmic trading operations. On the other hand, if such technology may replace human traders in the long run, where does that leave human autonomy and job opportunities?

In summary, while the development and the adoption of AI-driven algorithmic trading strategies in financial markets have benefited the industry with increased efficiency and liquidity, it also raises ethical concerns and potential societal impacts. It is crucial that we carefully monitor and regulate the impact of these tools in the financial industry to ensure their deployment is fair, unbiased, and mindful of the wider social implications.

6.19   What are the main challenges and advancements in the field of stress testing and scenario analysis for the evaluation of systemic risk and macro-prudential policy?

Stress testing is an essential tool for assessing the resilience of the financial system and evaluating risks to financial stability. It involves simulating a range of stress scenarios to test the ability of financial institutions and the financial system as a whole to withstand adverse events. Stress testing is a key element of macroprudential policy, which aims to mitigate systemic risks and promote financial stability.

However, stress testing is not without its challenges. One of the main challenges is the difficulty in designing stress scenarios that are both plausible and severe enough to capture a wide range of risks. Stress scenarios need to take into account not only the impact of specific shocks but also how shocks can interact and amplify each other. For instance, a rise in interest rates could trigger a sharp decline in asset prices, leading to losses for banks and other investors, which could in turn lead to a tightening of credit conditions and a decline in economic activity.

Another challenge is the data requirements for stress testing. Stress scenarios require a wide range of data, including historical market data, economic data, and data on financial institutions' balance sheets and risk exposures. However, some of this data may be difficult to obtain or unreliable, particularly during times of stress when data becomes scarce or distorted.

Advancements in stress testing and scenario analysis have been made in recent years in response to these challenges. One such advancement is the adoption of macroprudential models that incorporate a variety of risks and linkages between different parts of the financial system. These models provide a more comprehensive view of the risks facing the financial system and the impact of shocks on the economy as a whole. They also allow policymakers to test the effectiveness of different macroprudential policy tools in mitigating systemic risks.

Another advancement is the use of machine learning and artificial intelligence techniques in stress testing. These techniques can help to identify previously unknown risk factors and correlations and can provide more accurate predictions of the impact of stress scenarios on the financial system.

In conclusion, stress testing and scenario analysis are essential tools for assessing the resilience of the financial system and evaluating risks to financial stability. However, designing plausible and severe stress scenarios and obtaining the required data remains a challenge. Advancements in macroprudential models and machine learning techniques are helping to overcome some of these challenges and provide policymakers with a more comprehensive view of systemic risks.

6.20 How do you address the challenges of model risk and the validation of complex quantitative models in the context of ever-changing market conditions and regulatory requirements?

Model risk is the risk of financial loss arising from incorrect or insufficiently tested models. In the context of quantitative finance, complex models are designed to enable financial institutions to make informed business and investment decisions. Such models play a crucial role in risk management, pricing, valuation, and portfolio optimization in the financial world. The correct usage of models can provide a competitive advantage, while incorrect usage can lead to financial losses, regulatory penalties, and reputational damage.

To address the challenges of model risk, it is critical to establish a robust model validation framework that ensures models are fit for purpose, reliable, and comply with regulatory requirements. The following steps can be taken to address the challenges of model risk:

1. Model development and documentation: Models should be developed and documented according to a clear set of guidelines that detail the necessary model assumptions, input data requirements, model methodology, and output interpretation. Any changes made to a model should be documented, and the rationale for the changes should be explained.

2. Model validation: Model validation should be carried out by a team of independent experts who are knowledgeable in both the modeling techniques and the underlying financial instru-

ments. The validation process should test the model comprehensively, including rigorous testing of individual components of the model, broader testing of how the model performs under various market scenarios, and ensuring that the model is adequately robust to deal with different inputs.

3. Stress testing: Stress testing and scenario analysis should be conducted to assess the model's effectiveness under different market conditions. The use of historical data, Monte Carlo simulations, and other techniques can help validate models and ensure that they are resilient to a wide range of potential risks.

4. Regular review: Models should be reviewed on a regular basis to ensure that they remain relevant and effective. Market conditions can change quickly, and models that were once effective may no longer be relevant. Regular review enables updates and improvements to be made to the models in line with changing market conditions and regulatory requirements.

5. Model governance: Model governance should be established to ensure that models are appropriately designed, deployed, and managed. Model governance includes a continual process of model risk assessment, model performance monitoring, and model change management.

In conclusion, addressing the challenges of model risk requires a robust model validation framework that covers all aspects of model development, validation, and governance. The framework should be regularly reviewed and updated in line with changing market conditions and regulatory requirements.

Made in the USA
Monee, IL
02 January 2025

75938456R00115